AI

In

Education

Artificial Intelligence is reshaping how we teach, learn, and prepare for the future. This book explores how AI can transform education while keeping human values at the core.

Written by

ERIC LEBOUTHILLIER

AF722310

AcraPublishing | 2025 1st Edition

Preface

Education is the foundation of progress, yet the way we teach and learn is undergoing rapid transformation. Artificial Intelligence (AI) is no longer a futuristic concept; it is already present in classrooms, online platforms, and administrative systems worldwide. From personalized learning to predictive analytics, AI is opening new doors to innovation while also raising important questions about ethics, equity, and the future role of teachers.

This book was written to bridge the gap between theory and practice, helping educators, parents, policymakers, and lifelong learners understand both the opportunities and challenges of integrating AI into education.

Who this book is for

This book is designed for:

- **Educators and teachers** seeking to use AI to support student learning and reduce workload.
- **School administrators and policymakers** aiming to make informed decisions about adopting AI technologies.
- **Parents and guardians** who want to understand how AI impacts their children's education.
- **Students and lifelong learners** curious about how AI tools can enhance their learning journey.
- **EdTech entrepreneurs and innovators** looking to align their solutions with the real needs of classrooms.

What to expect from this book

Inside these chapters, you'll discover how AI is changing every layer of education—from classroom instruction to student support and school administration. You'll explore real-world examples of AI tools, strategies for effective adoption, and guidance on how to balance innovation with ethical responsibility. By the end, you'll have a clear vision of how AI can empower educators, personalize learning, and prepare students for the demands of an AI-driven future.

LEGAL DISCLAIMER

This publication is intended solely for informational and educational purposes. It does not constitute legal, financial, medical, or professional advice. The content is not a substitute for consultation with qualified experts or licensed professionals in the relevant fields.

Table of Contents

CHAPTER 1

The Evolution of Artificial Intelligence

The Evolution of Artificial Intelligence

Artificial Intelligence (AI) has become one of the defining forces of the 21st century. In education, it promises to reshape how we teach, how students learn, and even how we think about the role of schools in society. But to truly understand where AI is heading in education, we must first step back and trace its journey—from its conceptual origins in philosophy and early computing, to its present-day manifestations in generative AI and adaptive learning systems. The evolution of AI is not just a story of technological progress; it is a story of ideas, human ambition, and our ongoing quest to replicate, enhance, and partner with intelligence itself.

From Philosophical Questions to Early Machines

The roots of AI can be traced to ancient philosophy. Thinkers like Aristotle and Descartes asked fundamental questions: What is knowledge? Can reasoning be formalized? Could machines one day mimic thought? While these musings seemed abstract for centuries, they laid the intellectual groundwork for later breakthroughs.

The 20th century introduced the possibility of mechanizing intelligence. In 1936, Alan Turing proposed the concept of a "universal machine"—what we now call the Turing Machine—that could compute any mathematical problem given the right inputs. This theoretical foundation sparked the belief that machines could, in principle, simulate aspects of human reasoning. Turing's famous "Imitation Game," later known as the Turing Test, went further: if a machine could engage in conversation indistinguishable from a human, could we call it intelligent?

In the 1950s, this speculative thinking began to materialize. The Dartmouth Conference of 1956, often referred to as the birthplace of AI as a field, brought together pioneering researchers like John McCarthy, Marvin Minsky, and Herbert Simon. They declared that "every aspect of learning or any other feature of intelligence can in principle be so precisely described that a machine can be made to simulate it." While this bold vision underestimated the complexity of intelligence, it ignited a movement that continues today.

Early Machine Learning: Symbolic AI and Expert Systems

The first wave of AI research, stretching from the 1950s through the 1970s, was dominated by symbolic AI—systems that attempted to replicate intelligence by encoding rules and symbols. For example, early AI programs could solve algebra problems or play simple games like checkers by following carefully constructed sets of instructions. These rule-based systems seemed promising, but they had a major limitation: they could not handle ambiguity, unpredictability, or the richness of real-world human reasoning.

The 1980s saw the rise of "expert systems." These were AI applications designed to mimic the decision-making of human specialists in narrow domains, such as medical diagnosis or troubleshooting machinery. One of the most famous examples, MYCIN, was developed at Stanford to help doctors identify bacterial infections. Expert systems worked well when the rules were clear and limited, but they struggled as domains became more complex. Education briefly experimented with this approach through "intelligent tutoring systems," which attempted to guide students by applying sets of instructional rules. While useful in some settings, they lacked flexibility and failed to adapt to the nuances of individual learners.

These limitations led to what many call the "AI winters"—periods in the late 1970s and early 1990s when funding and enthusiasm for AI dwindled because the technology consistently fell short of expectations. Yet these winters were not the end of AI, but pauses that allowed new paradigms to emerge.

The Rise of Data-Driven AI and Machine Learning

The rebirth of AI came with the realization that intelligence could not be fully captured by rules alone. Instead, machines needed to learn from data. This shift gave rise to machine learning, where algorithms are trained to recognize patterns and make predictions based on examples rather than rigid rules.

In education, this paradigm shift opened the door to systems that could track student progress, identify weaknesses, and personalize recommendations. For instance, platforms like Carnegie Learning used machine learning to adapt math problems to each student's ability level. Instead of applying one-size-fits-all teaching methods, these systems used student data to shape instruction in real time.

The growth of the internet and advances in computing power during the late 1990s and 2000s accelerated this trend. Vast amounts of digital data—from online courses, student assessments, and even classroom interactions—became available for analysis. Machine learning could now process these datasets at scale, providing insights into learning behaviors and outcomes.

The transition from symbolic AI to data-driven AI was a turning point. For education, it meant moving from rigid systems to ones capable of adaptation, prediction, and personalization. This shift laid the foundation for the advanced AI tools we see today.

Deep Learning and the New Era of AI

The early 2010s marked another leap forward with the advent of deep learning. Inspired by the structure of the human brain, deep learning uses artificial neural networks with many layers to process information in increasingly complex ways. This approach has powered breakthroughs in image recognition, natural language processing, and speech recognition—technologies that underpin many of the AI tools now entering education.

For example, natural language processing (NLP) enables AI systems to understand and generate human-like text, which powers chatbots that can answer student questions instantly. Similarly, speech recognition allows language-learning apps like Duolingo to provide real-time feedback on pronunciation. Deep learning's capacity to analyze unstructured data—such as essays, voice recordings, or even classroom discussions—has expanded the horizons of educational AI far beyond what early systems could achieve.

In higher education, AI-driven plagiarism detectors now analyze billions of documents in seconds to identify originality. In K–12 classrooms, AI can assess student writing not just for grammar, but for clarity, argument strength, and creativity. These applications, fueled by deep learning, move education closer to providing personalized, real-time feedback at a scale once thought impossible.

Generative AI: A Paradigm Shift

While machine learning and deep learning improved pattern recognition and prediction, the arrival of generative AI represents a new paradigm altogether. Generative AI systems, such as GPT-4 or image-based models like DALL·E, do not just analyze data—they create new content. They can draft essays, generate lesson plans, design practice problems, or simulate complex scenarios for students to explore.

In education, this is a game-changer. Imagine a teacher needing differentiated reading passages for students at five different literacy levels. Instead of hours of preparation, a generative AI system can produce tailored texts in minutes. A student struggling with physics concepts can request multiple explanations until one resonates. A school administrator can use AI to model how schedule changes will affect teacher workloads and student outcomes.

Generative AI blurs the line between tool and collaborator. It offers not only efficiency, but also creativity—opening possibilities for more engaging, personalized, and innovative learning experiences.

Lessons from the Evolution of AI

Understanding the evolution of AI helps educators appreciate both its potential and its limitations. Every phase—symbolic AI, expert systems, machine learning, deep learning, and generative AI—has promised transformative change. Some promises have been realized, others overstated. The history reminds us of three critical lessons:

1. **AI progresses in waves, not straight lines.** Each breakthrough builds on past failures and successes. Education must prepare for cycles of rapid innovation and occasional setbacks.
2. **AI's impact depends on context.** Early expert systems struggled in education because they could not adapt to messy, human-centered learning environments. Newer tools succeed because they are designed with flexibility and personalization in mind.
3. **Human partnership remains essential.** Despite advances, AI has not—and likely will not—replace the teacher's role as mentor, motivator, and moral guide. AI's strength lies in augmenting human intelligence, not replicating it wholesale.

The Road Ahead

As we stand in the generative AI era, the question is no longer whether AI will shape education, but how. Its evolution shows a trajectory of increasing adaptability, creativity, and integration into human workflows. For schools, this means reimagining classrooms where AI supports—not supplants—human relationships.

The next chapters of this book will explore this intersection in detail: how AI is transforming teaching, personalizing student learning, reshaping assessment, and challenging educators to adopt it responsibly. But as we move forward, the lesson from AI's evolution is clear: growth in education will not come from adopting technology for its own sake, but from using it wisely, ethically, and in service of students.

Key Takeaway

AI's journey—from philosophical speculation to generative systems—reveals a story of ambition, adaptation, and resilience. In education, this history is not just background; it is a guide. By understanding where AI has come from, educators can make informed choices about where it should go. The evolution of AI is, ultimately, a reminder that growth in learning—human or machine—requires patience, iteration, and vision.

Defining AI in the Educational Context

Artificial Intelligence (AI) in education refers to the application of machine learning, natural language processing, and other intelligent systems to enhance how we teach, learn, and manage educational environments. Unlike the broad, futuristic notions often associated with AI, in the classroom it is far more practical: recommendation systems that suggest learning materials, adaptive platforms that adjust to student progress, or predictive tools that help teachers identify who needs extra support.

In this context, AI is best understood as a **supportive partner**—a set of tools designed to extend human capability rather than replace it. It can process vast amounts of data far faster than educators ever could, offering insights that guide instructional choices, highlight patterns of student behavior, and streamline everyday tasks.

AI's role in education is therefore twofold: to make learning more **personalized for students** and to make teaching more **efficient for educators**. Students can receive tailored guidance that fits their pace and style of learning, while teachers gain better visibility into progress, challenges, and opportunities for improvement.

As we move deeper into the book, we will explore exactly how these tools are reshaping education, from teaching practices and student learning to administration and institutional planning.

What AI Is—and What It Isn't

At its core, AI is the use of computer systems to perform tasks that typically require human intelligence. These tasks include recognizing speech, interpreting text, making predictions, and even generating original content. Unlike traditional software, which follows fixed instructions, AI systems are designed to adapt, improve, and sometimes even create.

In education, this means AI can:

- **Analyze** student performance data to identify patterns.
- **Personalize** learning content to match a student's strengths or weaknesses.
- **Automate** repetitive administrative and teaching tasks.
- **Generate** instructional materials or practice exercises.

However, AI is not a magic box that instantly "teaches" students or "fixes" education. It does not replace the human dimension of learning: curiosity, mentorship, empathy, or critical thinking. AI cannot replicate the motivational impact of a teacher who believes in a struggling student or the social learning that occurs when peers collaborate. Understanding what AI is *not* is just as important as knowing what it is, because misperceptions often lead to over-reliance or misplaced trust in the technology.

Breaking Down AI for Educators

For practical purposes, we can think of AI in education through three main categories:

1. **Predictive AI** – Systems that analyze data to forecast outcomes, such as which students are at risk of dropping out.
2. **Adaptive AI** – Tools that adjust learning pathways in real time based on student interactions, like adaptive math or reading platforms.

3. **Generative AI** – Models that can produce new content, such as drafting lesson plans, creating quizzes, or explaining concepts in multiple ways.

Each of these categories serves different needs within schools. Predictive AI helps educators allocate resources more effectively. Adaptive AI personalizes learning experiences. Generative AI enhances creativity and efficiency. By breaking AI down into these functions, educators can see not just what the technology does, but also how it fits into their professional goals.

Many educators already use digital platforms—online learning modules, learning management systems (LMS), or automated testing tools. So what makes AI different? The distinction lies in **adaptivity and autonomy**.

Traditional EdTech follows static rules. For example, a quiz app might mark answers as correct or incorrect and provide standard feedback. AI-powered assessment, by contrast, can go deeper: it may detect common misconceptions in a student's reasoning, provide hints tailored to that error, and even adjust future exercises to strengthen weak areas.

In other words, traditional tools are reactive—they respond to inputs with pre-programmed outputs. AI tools are proactive—they analyze, predict, and adapt based on patterns. This leap from static to dynamic technology is what makes AI transformative in education.

Making AI Understandable Through Examples

Let's imagine three classroom scenarios:

- **Predictive AI in Action:** A high school uses AI-powered learning analytics to monitor attendance, homework submissions, and quiz results. The system flags students whose engagement patterns match those of past students who struggled. Teachers receive alerts and can intervene early with support before failure occurs.

- **Adaptive AI in Action:** A middle school math platform analyzes a student's problem-solving steps, not just whether the final answer is correct. If a student consistently struggles with fractions, the system slows down the pacing, provides visual explanations, and gives extra practice until mastery is demonstrated.
- **Generative AI in Action:** A teacher preparing a history lesson asks an AI assistant to generate reading passages about the Industrial Revolution at three different reading levels: beginner, intermediate, and advanced. The teacher then chooses and edits the versions most suitable for her students.

These concrete examples show how AI functions differently from traditional digital tools. They also highlight an important truth: AI is not replacing teachers but extending their capacity to teach more effectively.

The Human-Centered Definition of AI in Education

From a human-centered perspective, AI in education can be defined as:

"A set of technologies that use data and algorithms to enhance teaching, personalize learning, and support educational decision-making, while keeping human educators at the core of the process."

This definition emphasizes three principles:

1. **Enhancement, not replacement.** AI strengthens human teaching rather than substituting for it.
2. **Personalization, not standardization.** AI adapts to individual learners instead of enforcing one-size-fits-all instruction.
3. **Support, not control.** AI informs decisions but does not override the professional judgment of educators.

By adopting such a working definition, schools can cut through the hype and frame AI as a tool in service of human growth rather than as a threat to it.

Why Clear Definitions Matter

The way we define AI in education has real consequences. Ambiguous or exaggerated definitions can lead to fear, resistance, or misuse. For example, if AI is framed as "teacher replacement," educators will understandably resist adoption. If it is described as "just another EdTech tool," administrators may underestimate its ethical implications.

A clear, contextual definition helps educators ask the right questions:

- How does this AI tool serve learning goals?
- What data does it use, and how is that data protected?
- How will this system support teachers rather than sideline them?

With clarity, schools can move from being passive adopters of flashy technology to thoughtful implementers of tools that genuinely improve learning.

The Risks of Over-Definition

At the same time, it is worth noting that definitions should remain flexible. AI is an evolving field, and locking in a rigid definition today could make us blind to future possibilities. Just as early definitions of "computers" once excluded personal laptops and smartphones, our current understanding of AI will likely expand in the years to come.

Educators must therefore balance precision with openness—anchoring AI in the present reality of teaching while staying adaptable to what new technologies may bring.

The Teacher's Role in Defining AI

Interestingly, the definition of AI in education should not be left solely to technologists or policymakers. Teachers themselves have a crucial role. They are the ones who will use the tools daily, see how they interact with students, and understand both their benefits and their limitations.

When teachers frame AI as a supportive partner rather than an external imposition, students are more likely to adopt it positively. For example, a teacher who explains that an AI tutoring app is "like having a helper who gives you extra practice when I can't sit beside you" helps normalize the tool without overpromising.

Thus, the cultural definition of AI in schools will emerge not just from official documents but from everyday classroom narratives shaped by educators.

Key Takeaway

Defining AI in education is about more than technical accuracy—it is about clarity, trust, and purpose. AI should be understood as technology that enhances teaching, personalizes learning, and supports decision-making, always with humans at the center. By grounding the definition in practical realities and human values, schools can build a foundation for responsible adoption.

AI vs. Traditional EdTech

For decades, educational technology—or EdTech—has been part of classrooms. From the overhead projector to the learning management system (LMS), schools have repeatedly adopted digital tools to modernize instruction. Yet as artificial intelligence enters the scene, many educators are left wondering: is this just another chapter in the EdTech story, or is it something fundamentally new?

The answer is clear: AI is not simply a continuation of EdTech. It represents a paradigm shift. While both are digital tools, their nature, capabilities, and impact on teaching and learning differ significantly. Where traditional EdTech digitizes instruction, AI personalizes it. Where EdTech follows fixed rules, AI adapts dynamically. And where EdTech supports efficiency, AI extends creativity and human insight. To adopt AI wisely, schools must first understand how it diverges from—and surpasses—the EdTech that came before.

The Nature of Traditional EdTech

Traditional EdTech refers to software, platforms, and devices designed to support teaching and learning in predictable, rule-based ways. Some familiar examples include:

- **Learning Management Systems (LMS):** Platforms like Blackboard, Moodle, and Google Classroom that help teachers post assignments, share resources, and manage grades.
- **Drill-and-Practice Apps:** Programs like Math Blaster or language flashcard apps that provide structured exercises.
- **Content Libraries:** Video or resource repositories such as Khan Academy or Coursera's early models, where all learners consume the same pre-produced material.
- **Automated Testing Tools:** Systems that score multiple-choice quizzes instantly but provide little diagnostic insight.

These technologies have been transformative in expanding access to content and streamlining logistics. For example, during the COVID-19 pandemic, EdTech platforms enabled continuity of learning when schools shifted online almost overnight. Google Classroom saw usage spike to over 100 million users, and video conferencing platforms like Zoom became classrooms' lifelines.

Yet the limitations of EdTech quickly became visible. Teachers still had to manually adapt content to different student levels. Students working through online modules received the same sequence regardless of individual progress. Automated systems provided results but rarely offered personalized guidance. Traditional EdTech digitized classrooms but did not fundamentally rethink them.

What Makes AI Different?

Artificial Intelligence differs in one key way: **it learns and adapts**. Instead of relying solely on pre-programmed rules, AI systems analyze data, recognize patterns, and make predictions. This means they can respond flexibly to learners, teachers, and contexts.

AI in education is marked by several distinctive capabilities:

1. **Adaptivity:** Tools like adaptive learning platforms adjust pacing, difficulty, and even instructional style in real time based on a student's progress.
2. **Prediction:** Learning analytics powered by AI can identify students at risk of falling behind before grades reflect the problem.
3. **Generation:** Generative AI systems create new instructional content—quizzes, summaries, differentiated reading passages—on demand.
4. **Interaction:** Natural language processing allows students to "converse" with AI tutors, asking questions and receiving explanations tailored to their needs.

This adaptivity and intelligence make AI categorically different from the rule-based systems of traditional EdTech. It moves technology from being a passive tool to being an active collaborator.

Side-by-Side Comparisons

To illustrate, let's look at three everyday classroom functions.

Assessment:

- *Traditional EdTech*: A quiz app instantly grades a multiple-choice test and displays a percentage score.

- *AI*: An AI-powered assessment tool analyzes student reasoning, flags misconceptions, and recommends specific follow-up exercises.

Content Delivery:

- *Traditional EdTech*: Every student watches the same video on algebra, regardless of prior knowledge.
- *AI*: An adaptive math app detects that Student A struggles with fractions while Student B excels, then delivers different problem sets to each.

Teacher Support:

- *Traditional EdTech*: An LMS organizes due dates, submissions, and grades.
- *AI*: A generative AI assistant drafts lesson plans at multiple difficulty levels, provides real-time insights into student engagement, and suggests interventions for struggling learners.

The difference is not only functional—it is philosophical. EdTech delivers efficiency. AI delivers personalization.

Case Study 1: Adaptive Math

DreamBox, an AI-driven math platform, provides a striking contrast to older EdTech.

- With **traditional software**, every student completes the same 20 problems, regardless of mastery.
- With **AI-driven adaptivity**, DreamBox analyzes each response in real time. If a student demonstrates mastery, the system accelerates. If a student struggles, it slows down, offers hints, or presents visual aids.

A study published in *Journal of Research on Technology in Education* found that students using adaptive AI platforms achieved significantly higher math gains than peers using non-adaptive programs. This reflects AI's defining advantage: responsiveness.

Case Study 2: Writing Feedback

Writing instruction demonstrates another divergence.

- **Traditional tools** like Microsoft Word's grammar checker flag spelling or punctuation mistakes.
- **AI tools** like Grammarly or Turnitin Revision Assistant evaluate clarity, coherence, tone, and argument strength. They don't just correct—they coach.

Students receive suggestions like "strengthen your thesis statement" or "clarify the connection between these paragraphs." Instead of surface correction, they get formative feedback that helps them grow as writers—something traditional EdTech was never designed to do.

Case Study 3: Language Learning

Language apps provide a final example.

- **Rosetta Stone**, a pioneer of EdTech, offered structured lessons, vocabulary drills, and pre-recorded dialogues. Feedback was minimal.
- **Duolingo today**, powered by machine learning, tracks patterns in student errors and adapts lessons accordingly. AI speech recognition now evaluates pronunciation, offering immediate feedback.

Students experience something closer to a live tutor: personalized pacing, adaptive challenges, and instant responses.

Why This Distinction Matters

Some might argue that the difference between EdTech and AI is technical, but for educators, it is deeply practical. The shift has implications in at least three areas:

1. **The Teacher's Role:** In EdTech-driven classrooms, teachers provide all personalization. With AI, personalization is distributed, freeing teachers to focus on mentorship, creativity, and socio-emotional learning.
2. **Student Experience:** EdTech delivers uniformity. AI delivers tailored experiences, increasing motivation by meeting learners at their level.
3. **Equity:** Traditional EdTech often reinforces inequities, with students who have strong support systems benefiting most. AI, when thoughtfully designed, can narrow gaps by providing individualized support to every student.

In short, confusing AI with EdTech risks underestimating both its potential and its ethical stakes.

Global Perspectives

Around the world, schools are already experiencing these differences.

- In **China**, adaptive AI platforms like Squirrel AI analyze vast datasets of student performance to personalize lessons for millions of learners.
- In **the U.S.**, Carnegie Learning uses AI to provide individualized math tutoring, with studies showing improved outcomes in low-income districts.
- In **Finland**, AI tools are being piloted to support immigrant students learning Finnish, adapting vocabulary practice based on real-time progress.

Traditional EdTech expanded access. AI is reshaping *how* that access is experienced.

The Convergence Challenge

Of course, the boundary between AI and EdTech is not always neat. Many traditional platforms now integrate AI features. Google Classroom, for instance, has begun testing generative AI feedback tools. Learning management systems are adding predictive dashboards.

This convergence can confuse educators. Is the tool genuinely AI-driven, or just rebranded EdTech with minor automation features? To navigate this, schools must ask sharper questions:

- What exactly does the AI component do?
- Does it adapt in real time, or is it static content dressed in AI marketing?
- What risks—privacy, bias, over-reliance—come with the AI features?

Key Takeaway

Traditional EdTech digitized learning; AI personalizes and transforms it. While EdTech provided structure and efficiency, AI introduces adaptivity, prediction, and generation. This difference is not academic—it changes how students learn, how teachers teach, and how schools make decisions.

As AI continues to merge with conventional platforms, the risk is treating it as "just another tool." But AI is not merely the next step in EdTech's evolution—it is a new paradigm. Recognizing this distinction is essential for educators to adopt AI responsibly and maximize its benefits while mitigating its risks.

Ethical Considerations from the Start

Artificial Intelligence in education promises efficiency, personalization, and innovation. But it also raises profound ethical questions. When algorithms influence what students learn, how they are assessed, or even how teachers allocate their time, the stakes extend far beyond convenience. Ethical considerations cannot be an afterthought. They must be the foundation of how schools, policymakers, and technology developers approach AI.

In the past, educational technology was often adopted with little reflection beyond cost and usability. But AI operates differently: it learns from data, adapts to users, and makes predictions that affect human lives. This means the choices we make about AI in education carry consequences for fairness, privacy, equity, and the very nature of learning.

Why Ethics Cannot Wait

Historically, new technologies in schools have been rolled out first, evaluated later. For example, during the rise of learning management systems, little thought was given to how data would be stored, who could access it, or how it might shape student behavior. With AI, this approach is dangerous.

Consider these examples:

- A predictive AI system flags a student as “high risk” for dropout based on attendance patterns and test scores. What happens if the label becomes a self-fulfilling prophecy, influencing how teachers perceive and treat the student?
- An adaptive platform collects years of detailed performance data. Who owns this data—the school, the student, or the private company? What if the data is sold or leaked?
- A generative AI tool produces personalized essays or practice problems. If the model was trained on biased data, does it

inadvertently reinforce stereotypes or exclude certain cultural perspectives?

These are not futuristic hypotheticals—they are present realities. Ethics in AI education is not about avoiding distant problems but about addressing immediate risks while technologies are still being adopted.

The Core Ethical Challenges

Four ethical dimensions stand out as particularly urgent in educational AI:

1. **Bias and Fairness**
   AI learns from data, and data reflects human societies—with all their inequalities. If historical data shows that students from certain backgrounds underperform on standardized tests, an AI trained on this data may predict failure for similar students in the future. This can reinforce, rather than reduce, systemic inequities.

In education, bias can manifest in multiple ways:

- Predictive analytics over-identifying minority students as "at risk."
- Language learning apps favoring certain dialects or cultural contexts.
- Essay-grading algorithms undervaluing creativity or nontraditional argument structures.

Bias is not only a technical issue but a moral one. Schools must ask: are we embedding historical injustice into the very tools meant to improve learning?

2. **Privacy and Data Ownership**
   AI systems thrive on data—student demographics, attendance, grades, even behavioral cues like time spent on a question or facial expressions during class. But students are

among the most vulnerable populations in society, and their data deserves special protection.

Questions of privacy loom large:

- How long is student data stored, and by whom?
- Can it be used for commercial purposes?
- Do students and parents have the right to delete their data?

In Europe, the General Data Protection Regulation (GDPR) provides some protections, but globally, many schools operate without clear policies. Ethical adoption means treating student data not as a commodity, but as a trust.

3. **Transparency and Explainability**
   One of AI's most challenging features is its "black box" nature. Complex neural networks can make predictions without human users fully understanding how. In education, this is problematic. If an AI system tells a teacher that Student X is "at risk" or that Student Y "should receive easier content," the educator needs to know why. Without transparency, teachers are left to either blindly trust or entirely reject the system.

Ethical AI in education must prioritize explainability. Teachers, students, and parents deserve to know how decisions are made, what data is used, and what limitations exist.

4. **Teacher and Student Autonomy**
   AI can make powerful recommendations—but should it? Education is not simply about efficiency; it is about human growth. If AI begins to dictate learning paths too rigidly, it risks reducing teachers to system operators and students to passive recipients.

The ethical challenge is to ensure AI empowers rather than disempowers. Teachers must retain professional judgment, and students must remain active participants in their own learning.

Case Studies of Ethical Dilemmas

Case 1: Predictive Analytics Gone Wrong
In a U.S. school district, a predictive model was deployed to identify students at risk of dropping out. Teachers were encouraged to intervene early. However, the model disproportionately flagged minority students, even when their performance was stable. Teachers, unconsciously influenced by the system, began lowering expectations for flagged students. Instead of supporting them, the AI reinforced harmful stereotypes.

Case 2: Data Privacy in Online Platforms
During the pandemic, many schools rapidly adopted EdTech platforms with AI features. Later, investigations revealed that some companies were tracking student data for targeted advertising. Parents were outraged to learn that their children's learning behaviors were being monetized without consent. The absence of ethical guardrails turned a tool of learning into a mechanism of exploitation.

Case 3: Automated Essay Scoring Bias
An AI-based writing assessment system rolled out across several schools promised efficiency in grading. However, it soon became clear that essays written in non-standard English received lower scores, even when the content was strong. Students who spoke dialects or English as a second language were unfairly penalized. The system saved time for teachers but harmed students most in need of fairness.

These examples highlight a truth: the risks of AI in education are not theoretical—they are here now.

Building Ethical AI in Education

How can schools address these challenges? The solution lies in proactive, principle-driven adoption. Some key strategies include:

1. **Establish Clear Ethical Frameworks**
   Schools and education ministries should create explicit guidelines for AI use. These frameworks should address fairness, transparency, accountability, and privacy. For example, UNESCO's *AI in Education* guidance emphasizes human rights and equity as non-negotiable principles.
2. **Require Human Oversight**
   AI systems should support, not replace, professional judgment. Teachers must remain the final decision-makers in instructional and evaluative contexts. If an AI suggests that a student is "falling behind," the teacher should interpret and contextualize that suggestion—not follow it blindly.
3. **Ensure Student and Parent Voice**
   Students and families deserve a role in decisions about AI adoption. This includes explaining how tools work, what data they collect, and what rights families have over that data. Transparency builds trust.
4. **Audit for Bias Regularly**
   AI systems must be tested and retested to ensure they do not systematically disadvantage certain groups. Independent audits, not just company claims, are essential. Schools should demand evidence of fairness before adoption.
5. **Prioritize Data Minimization**
   The principle of "collect only what you need" is vital. If a reading app can function without recording a child's location or unrelated browsing habits, it should not collect them. Data minimization reduces both risk and ethical burden.

The Global Picture

Different countries are grappling with AI ethics in education in different ways:

- **European Union:** The upcoming AI Act will regulate high-risk AI systems, including those in education, requiring strict transparency and accountability.
- **China:** Large-scale adaptive platforms raise questions about student surveillance, as massive amounts of data are collected for centralized analysis.
- **United States:** Regulations are fragmented, leaving school districts to make independent decisions about AI adoption, often without adequate expertise.
- **Finland:** Known for its progressive education system, Finland has prioritized human-centered AI, piloting tools only after rigorous ethical review.

These global contrasts reveal both risks and opportunities. Countries that build ethics into AI adoption from the start will likely lead in creating systems that enhance equity and trust.

The Educator's Responsibility

While policymakers and developers set frameworks, teachers are the front line of ethical AI. How they introduce, contextualize, and use these tools shapes student perception. A teacher who presents an AI platform as "a helper that gives you practice" encourages student agency. A teacher who frames it as "the system that will grade you" risks alienation.

Teachers must also cultivate **AI literacy**—not to become technologists, but to understand enough to ask critical questions. What data is being used? How are recommendations generated? Where might bias creep in? Ethical classrooms are led by educators who treat AI with both curiosity and caution.

Key Takeaway

AI in education is not just a technological issue—it is an ethical one. The stakes involve fairness, privacy, autonomy, and trust. If ethics are sidelined, schools risk reinforcing inequalities and undermining the very purpose of education. But if ethics are prioritized from the start, AI can become a powerful partner in creating more just, inclusive, and meaningful learning.

The lesson is clear: adopting AI without ethics is like building a school without a foundation. The structure may rise quickly, but it will not stand. For AI to truly serve education, ethics must not follow adoption—they must lead it.

CHAPTER 2

Transforming Teaching Practices

AI as a Teaching Assistant

Teachers are at the heart of education. They inspire, guide, and shape the intellectual and emotional growth of their students. Yet, teaching is also a profession burdened by administrative tasks, repetitive grading, and the constant demand to create new materials. Many educators spend as much time preparing lessons and marking assignments as they do engaging directly with students.

Artificial Intelligence has the potential to act as a powerful teaching assistant—one that never tires, never loses patience, and can process vast amounts of information instantly. But unlike human teaching assistants, AI does not seek to replace the teacher. Instead, it extends their capacity, giving them more time to focus on the aspects of teaching that are uniquely human: mentorship, encouragement, and the building of relationships.

The Overloaded Teacher

To appreciate AI's value, we must first understand the workload of teachers. Surveys consistently show that teachers work well beyond contractual hours. In the United States, the National Center for Education Statistics reports that teachers average over **50 hours per week**, with nearly half of that time spent on tasks outside of direct instruction—grading, lesson planning, data entry, administrative paperwork.

This imbalance leaves less time for the core of education: connecting with students. Many teachers describe feeling more like bureaucrats than mentors. Burnout is a growing concern, contributing to high attrition rates in the profession.

AI as a teaching assistant directly addresses this challenge. By automating repetitive tasks and offering real-time support, it allows teachers to reclaim their most valuable resource—time.

Grading and Assessment Support

One of the most time-consuming tasks teachers face is grading. Traditional EdTech tools automated grading for multiple-choice tests, but AI takes this further.

- **Automated Essay Scoring:** Modern AI systems can evaluate not only grammar and spelling but also coherence, argumentation, and creativity. For example, platforms like *Turnitin Revision Assistant* or *WriteToLearn* provide formative feedback on student writing. Teachers can then focus on higher-level coaching rather than correcting mechanics.
- **Formative Feedback at Scale:** AI can deliver instant feedback to students after each assignment, guiding them toward improvement before the teacher reviews the work. This reduces the feedback bottleneck while maintaining instructional quality.
- **Fairness through Consistency:** Unlike humans, AI does not experience fatigue or bias from grading hundreds of papers in one night. While AI systems require oversight to avoid algorithmic bias, they offer consistency that supports fairness in evaluation.

A teacher in a large high school might face grading 150 essays. With AI support, the teacher can spend less time marking errors and more time conferencing with students about ideas, interpretations, and critical thinking skills.

Lesson Planning and Resource Generation

Teachers spend countless hours preparing lessons, often reinventing the wheel each year. AI teaching assistants can ease this burden:

- **Customized Lesson Plans:** Generative AI tools can produce lesson outlines, differentiated activities, and even full slide decks tailored to specific grade levels, subjects, or learning standards.

- **Multiple Formats:** Teachers can request the same material in different formats—visual, auditory, interactive—so students with diverse learning preferences are all supported.
- **Adaptation for Diverse Learners:** AI can instantly modify materials for English language learners or students with learning disabilities, saving teachers hours of manual adaptation.

Imagine a teacher preparing a unit on photosynthesis. Instead of spending hours sourcing materials, they prompt an AI assistant: *"Create a 45-minute lesson on photosynthesis for 9th graders, including a hands-on activity and a short quiz."* The AI delivers a draft plan, which the teacher reviews, edits, and personalizes. What once took hours can now take minutes, leaving more time for reflection and creativity.

Administrative and Logistical Assistance

Beyond the classroom, teachers manage countless administrative tasks—recording attendance, sending reminders, responding to emails, entering grades into systems. AI can streamline many of these duties:

- **Automated Communication:** AI chatbots can handle routine student or parent inquiries (e.g., "When is the homework due?"), allowing teachers to focus on more meaningful interactions.
- **Scheduling and Organization:** AI-powered calendars can suggest optimal times for parent-teacher conferences, meetings, or grading sessions based on workload.
- **Data Analysis:** AI systems can track class performance trends, highlight which standards need more review, and suggest pacing adjustments.

These supports may seem small individually, but collectively they free teachers from administrative overload and restore focus on pedagogy.

Real-Time Classroom Support

AI is increasingly capable of providing live support during instruction:

- **Classroom Analytics:** Tools can monitor student engagement through participation, quiz responses, or even facial recognition (where ethically implemented). Teachers receive instant insights, such as which students are disengaged or which concepts require re-teaching.
- **Interactive Assistants:** AI voice systems can answer factual questions from students during class, reducing interruptions while keeping the teacher focused on higher-order dialogue.
- **Adaptive Grouping:** Based on performance data, AI can suggest groupings for collaborative work that balance strengths and weaknesses among students.

This type of "augmented teaching" enables real-time responsiveness that would otherwise be impossible in classrooms of 25–30 students.

Case Study: South Korea's AI Classrooms

South Korea, a global leader in EdTech adoption, has begun integrating AI teaching assistants into pilot schools. Teachers use AI platforms to handle routine grading and generate lesson variations. Early reports suggest teachers spend significantly less time on administrative duties and more time mentoring students. Importantly, teachers remain in control, but AI functions as a "co-teacher" that manages routine tasks.

A teacher interviewed by the *Korea Times* explained: *"I used to spend two hours each evening preparing lesson materials. With AI support, I can focus on designing projects and supporting students individually. It has given me back my role as an educator."*

The Human-AI Partnership

Despite its efficiency, AI must be framed carefully in schools. Teachers may fear replacement, while students may worry about losing human connection. The ethical and effective approach is to position AI as an assistant, not a substitute.

- **Teachers bring empathy, moral guidance, and inspiration.**
- **AI brings efficiency, adaptability, and scalability.**

Together, they form a partnership where each strengthens the other's weaknesses. Teachers are freed from drudgery, while AI is guided by human wisdom and values.

Risks and Limitations

AI as a teaching assistant is not without challenges:

- **Over-Reliance:** Teachers may become too dependent on AI-generated materials, reducing creativity or professional growth.
- **Bias in Grading:** Automated essay scoring systems may undervalue non-traditional writing styles or cultural expressions.
- **Data Concerns:** Administrative AI tools often require student data, raising privacy issues if not handled responsibly.
- **Equity Gaps:** Schools with fewer resources may not have access to advanced AI systems, widening inequalities.

Acknowledging these risks is essential. The goal is not blind adoption but thoughtful integration.

Building Trust with Teachers

For AI to function effectively as a teaching assistant, trust is crucial. Teachers must feel confident that AI tools respect their expertise and support rather than undermine them. Professional development is key: educators need training not only in how to use AI, but in how to evaluate it critically.

Schools should involve teachers in AI adoption decisions, gathering feedback and adjusting implementation. When teachers feel ownership, they are more likely to embrace AI as a partner.

Looking Ahead

As AI tools become more sophisticated, their role as teaching assistants will only grow. Future developments may include:

- AI systems that analyze classroom discussions to suggest follow-up questions.
- Tools that adapt lesson pacing in real time, adjusting based on student body language or response time.
- AI mentors for teachers themselves, providing instant access to best practices or suggesting new instructional strategies.

The horizon is exciting, but the foundation must remain human-centered. AI cannot replace the relational, emotional, and ethical dimensions of teaching. Instead, it should clear space for teachers to focus on these irreplaceable roles.

Key Takeaway

AI as a teaching assistant represents one of the most immediate and practical applications of artificial intelligence in education. By automating grading, streamlining lesson planning, supporting communication, and offering real-time analytics, AI can relieve teachers of administrative overload and restore focus to what matters most: relationships, mentorship, and the joy of learning.

The promise of AI is not that it will make teachers obsolete, but that it will make them more human. By partnering with AI, educators can reclaim their time, energy, and creativity—transforming classrooms into spaces where technology handles routine tasks and teachers inspire growth.

Adaptive Instructional Tools

One of the most profound contributions of artificial intelligence to education lies in adaptive instructional tools—systems that adjust what, how, and when students learn based on real-time analysis of their performance. For decades, teachers have dreamed of personalized learning, yet in classrooms of 25 or more students, true individualization has been almost impossible. AI makes this dream far more attainable by analyzing data at scale and delivering tailored learning experiences for every student.

Adaptive instructional tools move beyond static lessons and one-size-fits-all pacing. They act like an invisible tutor inside the classroom, observing how each student interacts with material, diagnosing strengths and weaknesses, and modifying instruction accordingly. Instead of delivering the same worksheet to thirty students, adaptive AI provides thirty different paths—each designed to challenge, support, and guide learners toward mastery

The Promise of Personalization

Education has long wrestled with a tension between standardization and personalization. Standardization allows systems to scale—students learn the same content, are tested by the same assessments, and are compared by the same metrics. Yet personalization is what truly drives engagement and mastery—students learn best when instruction matches their readiness, interests, and pace.

Traditional methods of personalization rely heavily on teachers. A skilled teacher might provide differentiated assignments, group students by ability, or offer one-on-one coaching. But these approaches are time-consuming and difficult to sustain in large classrooms. Adaptive AI tools expand personalization from a possibility to a reality, allowing every learner to receive tailored guidance without overwhelming teachers.

How Adaptive AI Works

At its core, adaptive learning relies on algorithms that collect and analyze student performance data in real time. The process can be broken down into four stages:

1. **Data Collection:** Every click, response, or hesitation provides information. Did the student answer correctly? How long did it take? Did they request a hint?
2. **Diagnosis:** The system interprets this data to infer the student's current level of understanding. For example, frequent errors on fraction problems suggest a conceptual gap.
3. **Adaptation:** Based on the diagnosis, the system selects the next step—an easier problem, a targeted explanation, or an acceleration to more advanced content.
4. **Continuous Feedback Loop:** As the student interacts further, new data refines the model, creating an ongoing cycle of personalization.

This loop allows AI to respond dynamically, much like a tutor observing a student's thought process and adjusting instruction on the spot.

Case Study 1: ALEKS

ALEKS (Assessment and Learning in Knowledge Spaces) is a well-established adaptive platform used widely in mathematics and science education. Unlike traditional software that presents the same set of problems to all students, ALEKS continuously maps what each learner knows and what they are ready to learn next.

For example, a student struggling with algebra may still excel at geometry. ALEKS identifies these nuances and builds individualized learning paths. In large university courses, professors report that ALEKS enables struggling students to catch up without slowing down advanced learners.

Research from McGraw-Hill (ALEKS's publisher) found that students using the platform were significantly more likely to pass gateway math courses compared to those in traditional instruction. The adaptive approach helps close gaps that often lead to failure in introductory college courses.

Case Study 2: DreamBox Learning

DreamBox Learning, an adaptive math program for K–8 students, demonstrates how personalization can improve engagement. The platform monitors not only right or wrong answers but also how students solve problems. If a student repeatedly guesses, DreamBox recognizes disengagement and adjusts with scaffolding or encouragement. If a student demonstrates mastery, it accelerates to prevent boredom.

Teachers using DreamBox report that it functions as a "silent partner." The system provides detailed dashboards showing each student's progress, allowing teachers to focus their attention on the students who need it most.

Case Study 3: Duolingo's Personalization

In language learning, Duolingo offers a familiar example. While it began as a fixed-sequence platform, its later versions incorporate AI-powered personalization. If a learner struggles with verb conjugation but excels in vocabulary, the app prioritizes exercises on verbs. Speech recognition AI provides real-time pronunciation feedback, offering individualized support once limited to one-on-one tutoring.

Duolingo's success illustrates the scalability of adaptive tools. With over 500 million users worldwide, it demonstrates that AI-driven personalization can reach learners at a scale never before possible.

Benefits for Teachers

Adaptive instructional tools are not designed to replace teachers but to complement them. Benefits include:

- **Targeted Intervention:** Dashboards highlight students at risk or concepts that require reteaching, helping teachers prioritize.
- **Data-Driven Insight:** Teachers gain a clearer picture of class-wide patterns and individual trajectories.
- **Time Reclaimed:** With AI handling repetitive practice and monitoring, teachers can focus on deeper engagement—projects, discussions, and mentoring.

A middle school teacher once explained: *"Before adaptive software, I had to guess who was really struggling. Now, the system tells me exactly which students need help with fractions, so I can spend my time working with them instead of spreading myself too thin."*

Challenges and Limitations

Despite their promise, adaptive tools raise important challenges:

1. **Data Privacy:** These systems rely on large volumes of student data, raising concerns about who owns it and how it is used.
2. **Algorithmic Bias:** If the underlying models are trained on limited datasets, they may misinterpret student performance, particularly for diverse learners.
3. **Over-Reliance on Technology:** Adaptive systems risk reducing learning to individual screen time, neglecting the social and collaborative dimensions of education.

4. **Equity of Access:** Schools with limited resources may not have access to high-quality adaptive platforms, creating further divides.

Addressing these challenges requires ethical design, transparency, and teacher oversight. Adaptive tools should serve as assistants, not drivers, of learning.

The Human Element in Adaptive Learning

It is crucial to remember that adaptation is not only about pacing—it is also about context, culture, and emotion. AI can detect when a student struggles with fractions, but it cannot sense the frustration in their tone of voice or the discouragement in their body language. Teachers remain essential in interpreting the human side of learning.

The best adaptive systems therefore include human-in-the-loop design, where AI provides recommendations but teachers make final decisions. This balance ensures personalization remains human-centered.

Global Adoption

- **China:** Companies like Squirrel AI operate large-scale adaptive systems serving millions of students. These platforms claim to deliver personalized lessons equivalent to one-on-one tutoring, though critics raise concerns about heavy surveillance and student autonomy.
- **United States:** Carnegie Learning combines AI with classroom teaching, offering blended learning environments where teachers use AI insights to shape lessons.
- **India:** Adaptive platforms are expanding access to high-quality education for students in rural areas, helping bridge gaps in teacher availability.

These cases demonstrate both the promise and complexity of adaptive learning. Its implementation reflects cultural values, resource availability, and policy priorities.

Looking Ahead

As AI technology advances, adaptive tools will become even more sophisticated:

- Systems will not only adapt content but also detect emotional states, adjusting encouragement and support.
- Platforms will integrate collaboration, suggesting peer partners for projects based on complementary skills.
- Adaptive learning will move beyond academic content to areas like social-emotional learning, career guidance, and life skills.

However, the central question will remain: how do we ensure that adaptation serves human growth rather than narrowing learning to what is most efficient to measure?

Key Takeaway

Adaptive instructional tools represent one of the clearest examples of AI's transformative potential in education. They move beyond static lessons to create personalized pathways that meet learners where they are. For teachers, they provide data-driven insights and relieve the burden of trying to differentiate instruction for dozens of students simultaneously.

Yet, their power must be balanced with ethical caution. Adaptive tools should augment, not replace, the human dimensions of teaching—empathy, encouragement, and cultural understanding. When implemented responsibly, they can make personalized learning not just a dream but an everyday reality for millions of students worldwide.

Enhancing Teacher Productivity

Teaching is one of the most demanding professions. Beyond classroom instruction, educators juggle grading, lesson planning, data entry, communication with parents, and administrative paperwork. Many teachers describe their roles as two jobs in one: the visible, inspiring work of teaching students, and the invisible, exhausting work of managing tasks that surround it.

Artificial Intelligence offers a solution—not by replacing teachers, but by enhancing their productivity. AI can automate repetitive duties, organize data more effectively, and provide instant insights, allowing teachers to reclaim time and energy for what matters most: building meaningful relationships with students and fostering deeper learning.

The Productivity Challenge in Education

To understand why AI-enhanced productivity is so vital, consider the numbers. In the United States, surveys show that teachers work an average of **50–55 hours per week**. Of this, only about half is spent in direct instruction. The rest goes to preparation, grading, meetings, paperwork, and administrative responsibilities.

Teachers in the United Kingdom report similar trends, with many spending evenings and weekends catching up on tasks. A 2019 survey by the UK Department for Education found that teachers worked an average of **54 hours a week**, with a large proportion of that time on non-teaching activities.

This imbalance has real consequences:

- **Burnout:** High workload is one of the leading causes of teacher attrition.
- **Reduced Focus:** Time spent on repetitive tasks detracts from planning engaging lessons or providing individualized support.

- **Equity Gaps:** Overwhelmed teachers may struggle to give attention to students who need it most.

By enhancing productivity, AI offers to reduce these burdens, enabling teachers to focus their expertise where it has the greatest impact.

Automating Administrative Tasks

One of AI's clearest contributions is the automation of administrative duties that consume teachers' time.

- **Attendance Tracking:** AI systems integrated into classroom platforms can automatically record attendance through digital logins or even facial recognition (where ethically implemented).
- **Grade Entry:** Instead of manually inputting scores into spreadsheets, AI can sync results directly into school databases.
- **Scheduling Assistance:** AI-powered calendars can suggest optimal times for meetings, conferences, or grading sessions, reducing the cognitive load of logistics.

For example, in Singapore, schools piloting AI-driven administrative systems found that teachers saved several hours each week previously spent on record-keeping. That time was redirected toward lesson planning and student support.

Streamlining Grading and Feedback

Grading is one of the most labor-intensive parts of teaching. Traditional EdTech automated grading only for multiple-choice exams. AI takes this further:

- **Essay Evaluation:** Platforms like *Turnitin Revision Assistant* or *Gradescope* use AI to provide instant feedback on student writing, identifying not only grammar errors but also structure, coherence, and argument strength.

- **Mathematical Problem Solving:** AI can evaluate step-by-step reasoning, not just final answers, giving students targeted feedback on errors.
- **Consistent Rubrics:** AI systems apply rubrics uniformly, reducing subjective inconsistencies that can creep into human grading.

While teachers still need to review and finalize grades, the AI reduces the heavy lifting, freeing teachers to spend their energy on higher-order evaluation.

Smarter Lesson Preparation

Lesson planning is another area where AI enhances productivity. Teachers spend hours searching for resources, creating slides, or writing practice questions. AI can dramatically shorten this cycle:

- **Content Generation:** Generative AI tools can create draft lesson plans, quizzes, or worksheets based on specific standards and grade levels.
- **Differentiation:** Teachers can request materials at multiple difficulty levels, ensuring accessibility for struggling learners and enrichment for advanced students.
- **Curriculum Alignment:** AI can cross-reference lessons with state or national standards, helping teachers ensure coverage without manual comparison.

Consider a teacher preparing a unit on ecosystems. With AI assistance, they can generate sample discussion questions, diagrams, and formative quizzes within minutes. Instead of spending hours gathering materials, the teacher focuses on refining the lesson to fit their students' unique needs.

Real-Time Classroom Support

AI tools can also function during live instruction to help teachers manage productivity:

- **Analytics Dashboards:** Real-time dashboards highlight which students are struggling, allowing teachers to adjust instruction on the spot.
- **Adaptive Grouping:** AI can suggest optimal group arrangements for collaborative work, balancing strengths and weaknesses.
- **Interactive Support:** AI chatbots embedded in learning platforms can answer student questions during class, freeing teachers to engage in deeper discussions.

This doesn't replace the teacher's role—it amplifies it. Instead of being pulled in multiple directions, teachers can focus on the highest-value interactions while AI handles routine monitoring.

Professional Development Through AI

Teacher productivity isn't just about daily tasks; it also extends to professional growth. AI-driven platforms are now offering personalized professional development pathways:

- **Skill Tracking:** AI systems identify which instructional strategies teachers use most and suggest new ones to expand their toolkit.
- **Micro-Learning Modules:** Short, targeted training resources are recommended based on classroom performance data.
- **Peer Comparisons:** Teachers can see anonymized benchmarks of how colleagues approach similar instructional challenges.

This personalization mirrors the adaptive learning students receive. Just as AI tailors lessons for learners, it can tailor professional development for teachers, making growth more efficient and relevant.

Case Study: IBM Watson in Teacher Support

In pilot programs, IBM's Watson AI has been used to analyze student performance data and provide teachers with actionable recommendations. For example, if a class shows widespread difficulty with a concept, Watson suggests alternative instructional strategies. Teachers reported that such tools allowed them to spend less time sifting through data and more time focusing on solutions.

Case Study: AI in Japanese Schools

In Japan, AI tools have been deployed to reduce teacher workload in middle schools. One program uses AI to analyze homework submissions and automatically categorize common errors. Teachers then receive summaries that allow them to focus their teaching on the most frequent challenges rather than manually reviewing each paper. Early studies show that this reduces grading time by nearly 40%.

Risks and Considerations

While AI has clear potential to enhance productivity, several risks must be acknowledged:

- **Over-Reliance:** Teachers may lean too heavily on AI-generated lesson plans, reducing creativity or professional autonomy.
- **Bias in Automation:** If AI grading tools are not properly calibrated, they may misinterpret creative responses or disadvantage non-traditional learners.
- **Privacy Concerns:** Administrative AI systems often require sensitive student data, necessitating strict protections.
- **Digital Divide:** Schools with limited resources may not access advanced AI tools, creating inequities in teacher workload.

Productivity gains must not come at the cost of quality, fairness, or teacher agency.

The Teacher-AI Balance

Ultimately, enhancing productivity is not about making teachers work harder but about helping them work smarter. AI should serve as a supportive partner, handling the routine so teachers can focus on the relational, creative, and critical aspects of teaching.

The most effective implementations keep teachers firmly in the driver's seat. AI suggests, organizes, and drafts—but teachers decide, refine, and lead. This balance ensures that productivity gains enhance, rather than erode, the professional identity of educators.

Looking Ahead

As AI evolves, teacher productivity tools will likely expand into areas such as:

- **Voice-to-lesson transcription**, where a teacher's spoken notes are automatically turned into polished lesson plans.
- **Predictive workload analysis**, warning teachers when grading or administrative burdens risk becoming overwhelming.
- **Integrated parent communication systems**, where AI drafts empathetic progress reports tailored to each child's situation.

The future of productivity in teaching is not about more hours worked, but about better use of hours available. AI has the potential to rebalance the teacher's role, ensuring their time is spent on what no machine can replicate: inspiring students.

Key Takeaway

AI enhances teacher productivity by automating repetitive tasks, streamlining grading, supporting lesson planning, and providing real-time classroom insights. These tools free educators to focus on their core mission: fostering curiosity, building relationships, and guiding students toward growth.

The ethical challenge is to ensure productivity gains do not compromise creativity, equity, or teacher agency. When used thoughtfully, AI offers not just efficiency, but empowerment—restoring teachers' time, energy, and passion for the work that drew them to education in the first place.

Professional Development Through AI

Teachers are lifelong learners. To be effective in a rapidly changing world, they must continually refine their instructional strategies, adapt to new technologies, and deepen their subject knowledge. Professional development (PD) is the system designed to support this growth. Yet, for many educators, PD has long been a frustrating experience—generic workshops, one-size-fits-all seminars, or occasional conferences that feel disconnected from the realities of daily teaching.

Artificial Intelligence offers a chance to reimagine professional development. Just as adaptive learning tailors instruction to students, AI can personalize growth for teachers. Instead of passive participation in predetermined sessions, teachers can engage with AI-driven systems that diagnose their strengths and areas for improvement, recommend relevant resources, and provide just-in-time support.

If AI can transform classrooms for students, it can equally transform professional development for teachers—making it more relevant, responsive, and empowering.

The Shortcomings of Traditional PD

Most teachers are familiar with traditional professional development models:

- In-service days with district-wide workshops.
- Mandatory sessions on broad topics (e.g., "integrating technology" or "classroom management").
- Occasional conferences that inspire but rarely lead to sustained change.

These formats have value, but they often suffer from several problems:

1. **Generic Content:** Sessions may not address individual teachers' actual needs. A new teacher and a 20-year veteran attend the same workshop, even though their challenges differ dramatically.
2. **Lack of Follow-Up:** Inspiration fades without ongoing support. Teachers often return from PD sessions with ideas but no time or structure to implement them.
3. **Time Burden:** Workshops often take teachers out of classrooms, adding to workload rather than reducing it.
4. **Limited Relevance:** PD designed at the district level may feel disconnected from the specific contexts of classrooms.

As a result, many educators see PD as a compliance exercise rather than a genuine growth opportunity.

How AI Reimagines Professional Development

AI changes the equation by enabling personalization, flexibility, and continuous learning. The same principles that drive adaptive instruction for students can support adaptive professional development for teachers.

Key features include:

- **Diagnostic Tools:** AI analyzes classroom data—student performance, teacher feedback patterns, lesson plans—to identify areas where teachers may benefit from support.
- **Personalized Learning Paths:** Instead of attending generic workshops, teachers receive targeted resources, micro-lessons, or coaching suggestions aligned with their needs.
- **On-Demand Support:** AI-powered platforms provide just-in-time guidance. For example, a teacher struggling with student engagement can instantly access strategies proven effective in similar contexts.
- **Progress Tracking:** Teachers can see their own growth over time, with AI recommending next steps based on demonstrated mastery.

Case Study 1: AI Coaching Systems

In the United States, pilot programs have experimented with AI-powered coaching platforms. One system records classroom sessions, transcribes teacher-student interactions, and provides feedback on factors such as teacher talk time, questioning strategies, or equity of participation. Teachers then receive personalized suggestions: ask more open-ended questions, distribute attention more evenly, or integrate more wait time after posing questions.

Unlike traditional PD, this feedback is immediate, specific, and tailored. Teachers describe it as having a "mirror" for their practice—one that helps them reflect and improve without judgment.

Case Study 2: AI in Teacher Training Colleges

In Finland, teacher training programs are beginning to integrate AI tools that simulate classroom scenarios. Prospective teachers practice responding to challenging situations—such as disruptive behavior or cultural misunderstandings—while AI provides feedback on tone, timing, and choice of strategy. This allows new teachers to practice in a safe, controlled environment before facing real classrooms.

These AI simulations are not replacements for field experience but powerful supplements, offering repeated practice that human mentors cannot always provide.

The Rise of Micro-Learning

One of AI's greatest strengths is delivering professional development in micro-formats. Instead of day-long workshops, teachers receive 5–10 minute modules targeted at a specific need. For example:

- A teacher preparing to introduce group projects receives a quick module on effective collaboration structures.
- A teacher noticing student disengagement can access a short guide on incorporating active learning strategies.
- An English teacher can receive AI-recommended exercises for scaffolding writing instruction based on student essay patterns.

This shift mirrors trends in other professions, where micro-learning and just-in-time training are replacing one-size-fits-all workshops.

Peer Learning Enhanced by AI

AI can also facilitate collaboration among teachers. Platforms can analyze data across schools or districts to identify common challenges and connect teachers with peers facing similar issues. For instance, if multiple teachers struggle with teaching fractions, the system might recommend forming a peer group, sharing strategies, and accessing targeted resources.

Such systems can also highlight "best practices" from high-performing classrooms, anonymized and shared across networks. AI thus acts as a bridge, amplifying the collective expertise of educators rather than isolating them.

Benefits for Teachers

The advantages of AI-driven professional development are significant:

- **Relevance:** Content aligns directly with classroom needs.
- **Efficiency:** Micro-learning modules fit into teachers' schedules.
- **Empowerment:** Teachers take ownership of their learning paths.
- **Sustainability:** Continuous, adaptive support replaces sporadic workshops.

Teachers who experience AI-driven PD often describe it as liberating. Instead of passively receiving information, they engage in a cycle of reflection, feedback, and growth tailored to their context.

Risks and Ethical Considerations

As with all AI applications, professional development tools come with risks:

- **Surveillance Concerns:** Classroom observation tools may feel intrusive if data is used for evaluation rather than growth. Teachers must trust that AI is a coach, not a monitor.
- **Equity of Access:** Wealthier districts may afford advanced AI systems, leaving others behind.
- **Over-Automation:** AI should support—not replace—human mentorship, which remains vital for nuanced feedback and emotional support.
- **Bias in Recommendations:** If AI bases suggestions on limited datasets, it may promote teaching strategies that ignore cultural or contextual differences.

Responsible implementation requires transparency, teacher consent, and safeguards to ensure AI remains a supportive tool, not a controlling one.

Global Outlook

- **China:** Large-scale AI platforms provide PD for teachers, though concerns arise about centralization and surveillance.
- **United States:** Districts like Dallas ISD are experimenting with AI-powered coaching to address teacher shortages and improve retention.
- **Europe:** Countries like Estonia and Finland emphasize ethical, teacher-centered AI use, focusing on empowerment rather than monitoring.

These global experiments reflect both the potential and pitfalls of AI-driven PD.

The Future of Teacher Growth

Looking ahead, AI may reshape teacher development in even more innovative ways:

- **Virtual Mentors:** AI avatars trained on expert teacher data could provide 24/7 coaching.
- **Predictive Growth Models:** AI could suggest future training needs based on patterns in a teacher's classroom.
- **Global Teacher Networks:** AI might connect teachers worldwide, translating languages in real time to foster international collaboration.

The key is balance: AI should enrich, not replace, the human dimensions of teacher learning. Mentorship, collegiality, and shared professional identity must remain central.

Key Takeaway

Professional development through AI offers a chance to finally make teacher growth personalized, relevant, and sustainable. By diagnosing needs, delivering targeted resources, and enabling peer learning, AI transforms PD from a generic requirement into a meaningful journey.

Yet the ethical stakes are high. If misused, AI could reduce professional autonomy or turn growth into surveillance. The future of PD depends on ensuring AI remains a supportive coach, not a controlling manager. When designed thoughtfully, AI gives teachers what they deserve: the same personalization, adaptability, and encouragement we want for their students.

CHAPTER 3

Personalizing Student Learning

Adaptive Learning Algorithms

Education has always grappled with a central challenge: how can a single teacher meet the diverse needs of dozens of students in a classroom? Every learner brings different strengths, weaknesses, and learning styles. Some grasp new concepts quickly, while others need more time and support. Traditional schooling often struggles to keep pace with this diversity, resulting in students who are either bored or left behind.

Adaptive learning algorithms—the backbone of AI-driven personalization—offer a powerful solution. By analyzing data in real time and adjusting instructional pathways, these algorithms make it possible to individualize learning at scale. They act like invisible tutors, tracking progress, diagnosing misconceptions, and tailoring instruction to each learner's unique profile.

The Science Behind Adaptive Algorithms

Adaptive algorithms are rooted in two main principles:

1. **Learning Analytics:** The continuous collection and analysis of learner data—such as response accuracy, time spent on tasks, and engagement patterns.
2. **Predictive Modeling:** Using patterns in the data to anticipate what a learner is ready for next, ensuring tasks are neither too easy nor too difficult.

For example, if a student takes unusually long to solve a math problem, the algorithm may infer uncertainty and adjust by offering a simpler problem or providing a hint. If another student answers quickly and correctly, the system escalates to more complex material. This constant feedback loop mirrors how a skilled tutor adjusts instruction based on observation.

Beyond Right and Wrong

Traditional assessments measure only correct or incorrect answers. Adaptive algorithms go further by analyzing the *process*. Did the student hesitate? Did they request help? Did they make the same error repeatedly? These micro-patterns provide a nuanced understanding of learning.

Consider a student solving algebra problems:

- Traditional grading would mark each solution as right or wrong.
- Adaptive algorithms might detect that the student consistently makes mistakes in distributing negative signs. The system responds by offering targeted practice and explanations specifically on that sub-skill.

This granularity allows adaptive platforms to pinpoint and address misconceptions in real time, preventing small gaps from becoming larger barriers.

Case Study 1: Knewton

Knewton, one of the earliest adaptive platforms, built algorithms that analyzed millions of data points to personalize instruction in math and reading. Its system continuously recalculated what each student knew and what they were ready to learn next. While Knewton faced commercial challenges, it pioneered the idea of "personalized pathways," demonstrating how adaptive algorithms could transform instruction from rigid sequences to fluid, individualized journeys.

Case Study 2: Carnegie Learning

Carnegie Learning, a U.S.-based math platform, combines cognitive science with adaptive AI. Its algorithms analyze not only correctness but also the strategies students use. For instance, if a student consistently guesses rather than reasons through problems, the system detects disengagement and adjusts by offering scaffolding or more guided practice.

Studies have shown that Carnegie Learning users outperform peers in traditional settings, especially in districts serving low-income students. The adaptive system helps close gaps that often widen under uniform instruction.

Case Study 3: Squirrel AI in China

China's Squirrel AI demonstrates the scalability of adaptive algorithms. Serving millions of students, it breaks content into micro-concepts and adapts learning pathways with extreme precision. If a student shows mastery of 85% of a topic, the system focuses only on the 15% remaining, optimizing efficiency.

While its approach raises questions about student autonomy and creativity, Squirrel AI illustrates how adaptive algorithms can be applied at massive scale, offering near one-on-one tutoring experiences in contexts where teacher-student ratios are overwhelming.

The Psychology of Adaptivity

Adaptive algorithms align closely with psychological theories of learning:

- **Zone of Proximal Development (Vygotsky):** Learning is most effective when tasks are just beyond a learner's current ability but achievable with support. Adaptive systems operate precisely in this zone, adjusting challenges to maintain optimal difficulty.
- **Flow Theory (Csikszentmihalyi):** Engagement peaks when tasks balance difficulty with skill. Too easy leads to boredom; too hard leads to anxiety. Adaptive algorithms help maintain this balance by calibrating content to each learner's level.

- **Mastery Learning (Bloom):** Students should achieve mastery of one concept before moving on to the next. Adaptive algorithms enforce mastery by detecting and remediating gaps before progression.

By aligning with these principles, adaptive systems not only personalize but also optimize learning.

Benefits for Students

The impact of adaptive learning algorithms on students can be profound:

- **Personalized Pacing:** Students progress at their own speed, preventing boredom or frustration.
- **Immediate Feedback:** Errors are identified and addressed instantly, accelerating mastery.
- **Increased Engagement:** Learning feels relevant and achievable, boosting motivation.
- **Equity:** Struggling learners receive additional support, while advanced learners are challenged.

For example, in a blended classroom using DreamBox, one student may practice visual fraction models while another tackles complex multiplication problems. Both are engaged at the right level, and neither feels held back or overwhelmed.

Benefits for Teachers

Adaptive algorithms also enhance teacher capacity:

- **Data Dashboards:** Teachers receive real-time insights into each student's progress and common misconceptions.
- **Targeted Intervention:** Instead of guessing who needs help, teachers can prioritize students flagged by the system.
- **Resource Allocation:** Teachers can spend less time on routine differentiation and more on mentorship and creativity.

A high school teacher once explained: *"The algorithm shows me which five students need support on quadratic equations today. That saves me hours of analysis and lets me give focused attention where it's needed most."*

Risks and Challenges

Despite their promise, adaptive algorithms raise important concerns:

1. **Data Privacy:** Continuous monitoring requires vast amounts of student data, raising questions about ownership and security.
2. **Bias in Algorithms:** If training data reflects inequalities, adaptive systems may reinforce them. For example, predicting low potential for students from certain backgrounds could limit opportunities.
3. **Over-Individualization:** Excessive personalization risks isolating students, reducing opportunities for collaboration and shared learning.
4. **Narrow Focus:** Algorithms may prioritize efficiency in mastering discrete skills but overlook creativity, critical thinking, or socio-emotional growth.

These risks highlight the need for human oversight. Adaptive systems must be tools, not replacements, ensuring teachers remain central in interpreting and contextualizing data.

Ethical Implementation

To adopt adaptive algorithms responsibly, schools should:

- **Ensure Transparency:** Teachers and students should understand how recommendations are generated.
- **Prioritize Privacy:** Collect only necessary data and protect it rigorously.
- **Balance Personalization with Collaboration:** Adaptive tools should complement, not replace, group learning experiences.

- **Audit for Bias:** Regular reviews must ensure algorithms serve all students equitably.

When ethical safeguards are in place, adaptive algorithms can support both personalization and justice in education.

Global Trends

- **United States:** Universities and K–12 districts increasingly use adaptive systems in math and science courses, improving retention in STEM fields.
- **China:** Large-scale adoption reflects a national push for efficiency but raises questions about creativity and holistic development.
- **India:** Adaptive platforms are expanding access to quality education in rural areas where teacher shortages are acute.
- **Europe:** Countries like Finland emphasize balanced adoption, ensuring adaptive learning complements, rather than dominates, pedagogical approaches.

These global patterns illustrate that while adaptive algorithms are universally promising, cultural and ethical contexts shape how they are applied.

The Future of Adaptive Algorithms

Looking ahead, adaptive learning algorithms are likely to evolve in three key directions:

1. **Emotion Recognition:** Using voice and facial analysis, systems may detect frustration or disengagement and adjust accordingly.
2. **Collaborative Adaptivity:** Algorithms may not only personalize for individuals but also optimize group dynamics, pairing students strategically.
3. **Holistic Learning:** Future systems may extend beyond academics to adapt lessons based on socio-emotional skills, creativity, and real-world problem solving.

The future is not just about smarter algorithms but about broader definitions of learning that AI can support.

Key Takeaway

Adaptive learning algorithms represent the engine of AI-powered personalization. By diagnosing needs, adjusting pathways, and providing continuous feedback, they bring individualized learning to scale. For students, they offer motivation, equity, and mastery. For teachers, they provide insights and efficiency.

But these benefits come with risks—privacy concerns, bias, and the danger of over-individualization. The solution is balance: algorithms should serve as guides, not gatekeepers, with teachers remaining the interpreters of data and the architects of learning.

In the end, adaptive learning algorithms are not about replacing teachers but about enabling them to do what they do best: connect with students, inspire curiosity, and guide human growth.

AI-Driven Tutoring Systems

Imagine every student having access to a patient, knowledgeable tutor available 24/7. This vision, once impossible due to cost and scale, is becoming reality through AI-driven tutoring systems. These platforms provide personalized support outside the classroom, offering explanations, practice, and encouragement at a level of accessibility no human tutoring system could achieve.

AI tutoring systems do not replace teachers or professional tutors. Instead, they extend learning opportunities beyond school walls, ensuring students can access help when they need it most—whether at home doing homework, revising for exams, or catching up on missed lessons.

The Tutoring Gap

Research consistently shows the power of one-on-one tutoring. The famous meta-analysis by Benjamin Bloom in the 1980s found that students receiving individual tutoring performed **two standard deviations better** than peers in traditional classrooms—a phenomenon known as the "2 Sigma Problem." Personalized tutoring produced outcomes equivalent to moving an average student into the top 2% of their class.

The problem has always been scale. Providing every student with a personal tutor is financially and logistically impossible for most school systems. Private tutoring industries thrive, but they are often limited to wealthier families, exacerbating educational inequities.

AI-driven tutoring systems address this gap by offering affordable, scalable alternatives that bring aspects of one-on-one support to all learners.

How AI Tutoring Works

AI tutoring systems function by combining several key components:

1. **Knowledge Bases:** Vast repositories of subject content, from math problems to grammar rules.
2. **Adaptive Algorithms:** Systems that diagnose student strengths and weaknesses in real time.
3. **Natural Language Processing (NLP):** Enabling conversational interactions where students can ask questions in plain language.
4. **Feedback Loops:** Providing explanations, hints, and additional practice based on student performance.

When a student struggles with a problem, the AI tutor doesn't just mark it wrong. It analyzes the error, provides tailored hints, and adjusts the next problem to build the missing skill. Some systems can even simulate the dialogue of a human tutor, asking guiding questions rather than providing answers outright.

Case Study 1: Khanmigo (Khan Academy)

In 2023, Khan Academy launched **Khanmigo**, an AI-powered tutor built on top of OpenAI's GPT models. Unlike static video lessons, Khanmigo engages in back-and-forth dialogue. If a student asks, *"I don't understand quadratic equations,"* Khanmigo responds with guiding questions, step-by-step hints, or multiple explanations.

Teachers can also use Khanmigo to generate practice problems, lesson variations, and even role-playing exercises. The platform exemplifies how AI tutoring supports both students and educators in real time.

Case Study 2: Carnegie Mellon's ITS

Carnegie Mellon University has pioneered **Intelligent Tutoring Systems (ITS)** for decades. These systems break down subjects into micro-skills and track student mastery. In math, for example, ITS identifies specific sub-skills like "simplifying fractions" or "solving for x" and adapts lessons accordingly.

Studies show ITS students often perform as well as those receiving human tutoring, particularly in structured domains like mathematics and computer science.

Case Study 3: Duolingo Max

In language learning, Duolingo's premium service, **Duolingo Max**, integrates generative AI to provide conversational practice. Learners can role-play real-world scenarios—ordering food, asking for directions—and receive real-time corrections. Unlike traditional flashcard-based apps, this feels like interacting with a live language partner.

Such innovations demonstrate how AI tutoring systems can make practice more engaging and contextual.

Benefits for Students

AI-driven tutoring systems provide several unique advantages:

- **Accessibility:** Available anytime, anywhere—no scheduling or travel required.
- **Affordability:** Often free or far cheaper than private tutoring, making support more equitable.
- **Personalization:** Adjusting explanations, examples, and practice problems to individual needs.
- **Confidence Building:** Students can ask "silly" questions without fear of judgment, encouraging curiosity.
- **Scaffolding Independence:** By offering hints rather than direct answers, AI tutors help students develop problem-solving skills.

For a student struggling late at night before a test, an AI tutor offers instant support that no teacher or parent may be available to provide.

Benefits for Teachers

Teachers also benefit from AI tutoring systems:

- **Homework Support:** AI tutors reduce the burden of students arriving to class confused, as many issues are resolved during independent study.
- **Data Insights:** Teachers can see which concepts students struggled with during AI tutoring sessions, informing future instruction.
- **Extended Reach:** Teachers cannot provide one-on-one help to every student outside school hours. AI tutors extend their support beyond the classroom.

One middle school teacher explained: *"When my students use AI tutors, they come to class with fewer gaps. I can focus on higher-level discussions instead of reteaching basics over and over."*

Risks and Concerns

While promising, AI tutoring systems also pose risks:

1. **Accuracy of Explanations:** Generative AI can sometimes produce errors or misleading explanations, requiring teacher oversight.
2. **Over-Reliance:** Students may depend too heavily on AI tutors, reducing persistence and critical thinking.
3. **Equity of Access:** While cheaper than private tutoring, AI systems still require devices and internet access—barriers for some students.
4. **Data Privacy:** Detailed records of student learning raise concerns about who owns and uses the data.

Addressing these risks requires transparency, human oversight, and equitable access initiatives.

The Role of Human Tutors

Importantly, AI tutors do not eliminate the need for human tutors. Empathy, encouragement, and motivational strategies remain uniquely human strengths. Instead, AI tutors can handle routine practice and foundational explanations, allowing human tutors to focus on higher-order thinking, emotional support, and confidence building.

Some hybrid models are emerging where AI provides basic instruction, and human tutors review progress and coach students on broader skills. This blended approach combines scalability with human connection.

Global Perspectives

- **China:** AI tutoring platforms like Zuoyebang provide massive after-school support, serving millions of students. However, concerns about screen time and data collection are significant.
- **United States:** Khan Academy and Carnegie Mellon lead innovations, with growing interest from school districts seeking to reduce inequities.
- **India:** AI tutoring apps are expanding rapidly in low-resource contexts, offering affordable alternatives where qualified human tutors are scarce.
- **Europe:** Countries like Estonia emphasize careful integration, ensuring AI tutoring supplements formal education rather than replacing teacher guidance.

These global experiments highlight both opportunities and challenges, reminding us that context matters in adoption.

The Future of AI Tutoring

Looking forward, AI tutoring systems are likely to evolve in powerful ways:

- **Emotional Intelligence:** Future tutors may detect frustration or boredom and adjust tone or pacing.
- **Multi-Modal Support:** Combining text, voice, and video explanations for diverse learners.
- **Cultural Adaptation:** Tutors trained on local contexts, examples, and languages for greater inclusivity.
- **Integration with Classrooms:** AI tutors may sync directly with teacher lesson plans, reinforcing content seamlessly.

The future of tutoring is not one-size-fits-all but many-sized-for-each, where every learner has support tailored to their needs.

Key Takeaway

AI-driven tutoring systems represent one of the most exciting frontiers in education. They make one-on-one support accessible at scale, offering personalization, affordability, and flexibility. For students, they provide confidence and independence. For teachers, they extend reach and reduce workload.

But these tools must be implemented with care. Without safeguards, they risk misinformation, over-reliance, or inequitable access. When balanced with teacher oversight and human empathy, AI tutors can close one of education's most persistent gaps: ensuring every learner has access to the support they need, when they need it.

Gamification Powered by AI

Play has always been a powerful way to learn. Children explore the world through games, and adults often remember best when knowledge is tied to fun, challenge, or reward. In education, "gamification" refers to the use of game elements—points, levels, challenges, rewards—to increase motivation and engagement in learning.

While gamification itself is not new, artificial intelligence takes it to an entirely new level. Instead of static points and badges, AI-powered gamification adapts in real time to each learner's preferences, behaviors, and performance. It transforms game-based learning from a generic experience into a personalized journey that keeps students motivated and challenged without overwhelming them.

Why Gamification Matters

Traditional education often struggles with motivation. Students may understand *why* learning matters, but the process can feel abstract, repetitive, or disconnected from their lives. Gamification addresses this problem by leveraging principles of psychology:

- **Immediate Feedback:** Just as games provide instant responses to actions, gamification offers immediate signals of progress.
- **Progression:** Levels and milestones create a sense of advancement.
- **Challenge and Reward:** Balanced difficulty keeps learners in a state of flow, where tasks are engaging but not frustrating.
- **Autonomy:** Games give players choices, which increases intrinsic motivation.

When these principles are applied to learning, students become active participants rather than passive receivers.

The Role of AI in Gamification

Traditional gamified platforms offer the same rewards and challenges to all students: complete a worksheet, earn a badge; pass a quiz, unlock a new level. While effective initially, this approach often loses impact because it does not adapt to individual learners.

AI changes this by personalizing gamification:

1. **Adaptive Difficulty:** AI adjusts challenge levels based on performance, ensuring learners remain engaged but not overwhelmed.
2. **Personalized Rewards:** Systems analyze student preferences to deliver rewards that are most motivating (e.g., narrative progression for one student, visual badges for another).

3. **Dynamic Narratives:** AI generates evolving storylines that respond to student choices, making learning feel like a personalized adventure.
4. **Behavioral Insights:** By tracking engagement patterns, AI can predict when motivation is waning and intervene with new challenges or incentives.

This level of personalization makes gamified learning sustainable over time, not just a temporary novelty.

Case Study 1: Classcraft

Classcraft transforms classroom management into a role-playing game. Students create characters, earn points for positive behaviors, and work together in teams. AI integration enhances this system by adapting rewards and challenges to student engagement levels. For example, if a student shows declining participation, the AI might increase incentives or offer tailored missions.

Teachers report that Classcraft not only boosts academic engagement but also strengthens classroom culture, as students collaborate in teams to achieve shared goals.

Case Study 2: Duolingo

Duolingo is one of the most famous examples of gamification in learning. Points, streaks, and leaderboards motivate millions of users worldwide to practice languages daily. AI personalization takes Duolingo further: the system adapts exercises based on learner errors, ensuring that progress is both engaging and effective.

The platform also experiments with personalized streak rewards and challenges, ensuring that learners stay motivated even when enthusiasm dips. For example, if a user misses several days, AI may generate a special challenge to reignite commitment.

Case Study 3: Minecraft Education Edition

Minecraft Education Edition allows teachers to use the popular game as a platform for learning subjects ranging from history to coding. With AI enhancements, Minecraft can analyze student interactions in-game and adapt challenges accordingly. For instance, if a student struggles with a building task related to geometry, the system might offer hints or simplify steps.

This blend of open-world exploration and AI-driven adaptation makes learning immersive and flexible.

The Psychology of AI Gamification

AI-powered gamification aligns with key psychological theories:

- **Self-Determination Theory (Deci & Ryan):** Motivation thrives when learners experience autonomy, competence, and relatedness. AI gamification supports autonomy through choices, competence through adaptive challenges, and relatedness through collaborative missions.
- **Flow Theory (Csikszentmihalyi):** Engagement peaks when challenge matches skill. AI ensures this balance dynamically by analyzing performance in real time.
- **Behavioral Reinforcement:** Personalized rewards strengthen positive learning behaviors, making persistence more likely.

By embedding these principles into adaptive systems, AI transforms gamification from surface-level fun into deep motivational design.

Benefits for Students

The impact of AI-powered gamification on students includes:

- **Sustained Motivation:** Dynamic rewards keep learners engaged longer than static systems.

- **Increased Mastery:** Adaptive difficulty ensures concepts are learned deeply before moving on.
- **Confidence Growth:** Achievements and progress tracking build self-efficacy.
- **Collaboration:** Multiplayer gamification fosters teamwork and peer learning.

For struggling students, gamification can turn frustration into progress. Completing small, adaptive challenges builds momentum, transforming failure into a manageable step toward growth.

Benefits for Teachers

Gamification supported by AI also benefits teachers:

- **Classroom Management:** Positive behaviors are rewarded in real time, reducing disciplinary issues.
- **Data Insights:** AI tracks engagement metrics, helping teachers identify when motivation is dipping.
- **Instructional Support:** Teachers can align game challenges with curriculum goals, ensuring fun serves learning.

A teacher using Classcraft explained: *"I spend less time managing behavior and more time teaching. Students are motivated to participate because the game rewards them for contributing."*

Risks and Limitations

While powerful, AI gamification comes with risks:

1. **Overemphasis on Rewards:** Students may become motivated only by external rewards, undermining intrinsic motivation.
2. **Equity Concerns:** Not all students respond equally to game mechanics; cultural and individual differences matter.
3. **Screen Time Issues:** Gamified systems can increase time on devices, raising health and balance concerns.

4. **Data Privacy:** Tracking motivation and behavior generates sensitive data that must be safeguarded.

Educators must balance gamification with broader pedagogical strategies to ensure it enhances, rather than dominates, learning.

Ethical Considerations

Gamification walks a fine line between motivation and manipulation. Ethical implementation requires transparency: students should understand why challenges and rewards are structured as they are. Teachers should use gamification as a tool to empower learners, not to coerce compliance.

AI intensifies this challenge because its personalization can make gamification extremely persuasive. Safeguards are necessary to ensure motivation remains genuine and healthy.

The Future of AI Gamification

Looking forward, gamification powered by AI may evolve in exciting ways:

- **Emotion-Aware Games:** Systems that detect frustration or excitement and adjust gameplay accordingly.
- **Narrative Generation:** AI-driven storylines that adapt to each student's choices, creating unique learning adventures.
- **Cross-Subject Integration:** Gamification spanning subjects, where progress in math influences storylines in history or science.
- **Mixed Reality Learning:** Combining AI with VR/AR to create immersive, adaptive game worlds tied to curriculum goals.

The next decade could see classrooms where students embark on collaborative quests spanning multiple disciplines, guided by adaptive AI that keeps each learner challenged and engaged.

Key Takeaway

Gamification has always been a powerful motivator, but AI takes it to new heights. By personalizing challenges, rewards, and narratives, AI-powered gamification sustains engagement, builds confidence, and aligns motivation with learning goals.

The risk is turning education into mere entertainment or manipulation. The opportunity is transforming classrooms into spaces where curiosity and challenge are as engaging as any game. With careful, ethical design, AI gamification can make learning not just effective, but irresistible.

Inclusive Learning for All

Education is built on the principle that every learner deserves the opportunity to thrive. Yet, for millions of students worldwide, traditional classrooms have been spaces of exclusion rather than inclusion. Learners with disabilities, language barriers, or unique learning needs often encounter obstacles that limit their participation and success.

Artificial Intelligence holds enormous promise for making education more inclusive. Through adaptive tools, accessibility technologies, and personalized supports, AI can help dismantle barriers that have historically left many students behind. However, inclusion through AI is not automatic—it requires thoughtful design, ethical safeguards, and collaboration between technologists, educators, and communities.

The Historical Challenge of Inclusion

For decades, schools have struggled to provide truly inclusive learning. Even well-intentioned systems often fail to meet diverse needs:

- Students with dyslexia may be penalized in reading-heavy curricula.
- Learners with hearing impairments may miss critical classroom dialogue.
- Non-native speakers may struggle with language-based instruction.
- Students with autism may find traditional teaching styles overwhelming.

Teachers do their best, but the scale of needs often exceeds available resources. Specialized support staff, like speech therapists or learning aides, are not always accessible—particularly in underfunded or rural schools.

AI tools offer scalable solutions that can provide individualized support without requiring one specialist per student.

AI for Students with Disabilities

AI is already transforming accessibility for learners with disabilities:

- **Speech Recognition for the Hearing Impaired:** AI-powered captioning systems like Microsoft's *Live Captions* or Google's *Transcribe* provide real-time text for spoken lessons, ensuring hearing-impaired students can fully participate.
- **Text-to-Speech for Dyslexia:** Tools like *Natural Reader* or *Kurzweil 3000* read aloud digital text, supporting students who struggle with reading fluency. AI algorithms can even adjust voice tone and pacing for comprehension.
- **Computer Vision for the Visually Impaired:** Apps like *Seeing AI* from Microsoft use AI to describe objects, people,

and text through audio narration, enabling visually impaired students to navigate classrooms and digital content.
- **Predictive Tools for Physical Disabilities:** AI-powered interfaces allow students with mobility challenges to control computers using voice, gestures, or even eye-tracking.

These tools empower students to engage more fully in the classroom, leveling the playing field by removing physical and cognitive barriers.

Case Study 1: AI in Dyslexia Support

In the UK, AI-driven reading assistants have been deployed to support students with dyslexia. These tools analyze patterns in reading errors and adapt exercises accordingly. Rather than generic practice, students receive targeted instruction that addresses their specific challenges. Teachers report significant improvements in reading fluency and student confidence.

Case Study 2: AI Captioning in Higher Education

At the University of Toronto, AI captioning tools have been integrated into lecture halls, providing instant subtitles for all spoken content. Originally designed for hearing-impaired students, captions have also proven useful for non-native English speakers, students with auditory processing challenges, and those reviewing notes after class. This illustrates how AI inclusivity tools often create universal benefits.

Supporting Neurodiverse Learners

AI also holds promise for students with autism, ADHD, and other neurodiverse conditions.

- **Emotion Recognition:** Some AI tools can detect signs of frustration, confusion, or disengagement through facial or voice analysis, prompting teachers to intervene early.

- **Structured Routines:** AI platforms can provide consistent, predictable schedules for students who thrive on routine.
- **Attention Support:** Adaptive platforms adjust pacing based on student focus, offering breaks or gamified tasks when attention wanes.

These supports respect neurodiverse learners' needs while integrating them more fully into mainstream classrooms.

Inclusive Language Learning

Language barriers are another major source of exclusion. AI offers breakthroughs in translation and multilingual support:

- **Real-Time Translation:** Apps like Google Translate and Microsoft Translator can provide instant speech-to-text translation, enabling multilingual classrooms to function more smoothly.
- **Adaptive Vocabulary Tools:** AI platforms identify gaps in second-language acquisition and deliver targeted practice.
- **Pronunciation Coaching:** Speech recognition AI provides personalized feedback for language learners, something teachers cannot scale individually.

For immigrant and refugee students, such tools make the difference between isolation and active participation.

Global Perspectives

- **India:** AI reading apps support rural students learning in local dialects, bridging gaps in teacher availability.
- **China:** Large-scale adaptive platforms include accessibility features for students with disabilities, though concerns remain about surveillance.
- **Africa:** AI tools on low-cost smartphones are expanding access to literacy for students who lack traditional resources.

Globally, AI is helping to bring inclusion to contexts where traditional resources are limited or nonexistent.

Benefits for Teachers

Inclusive AI tools are not just for students—they also empower teachers:

- **Personalized Dashboards:** Teachers can see detailed data on how students with special needs are progressing, allowing targeted interventions.
- **Differentiation at Scale:** AI automates the creation of multiple versions of the same material—simplified, visual, or auditory—without hours of extra preparation.
- **Reduced Dependence on Specialists:** While human expertise remains essential, AI supplements gaps where specialists are unavailable.

Teachers report feeling more confident in their ability to meet diverse needs when AI tools are integrated thoughtfully.

Risks and Ethical Concerns

While AI promises inclusion, it also carries risks:

1. **Bias in Accessibility Tools:** Speech recognition systems may perform poorly with non-standard accents, disadvantaging some learners.
2. **Privacy:** Tools analyzing emotions or behaviors raise sensitive concerns about surveillance, especially for neurodiverse students.
3. **Over-Reliance:** Schools may adopt AI as a cost-saving measure, reducing investment in human specialists.
4. **Digital Divide:** Students in low-resource contexts may lack access to devices or internet, limiting the reach of inclusive AI tools.

These risks highlight that inclusion requires more than technology—it requires ethical frameworks and investment in equitable access.

The Future of Inclusive AI

The next generation of AI inclusivity tools may include:

- **Emotionally Intelligent Tutors:** Systems that respond with empathy to student frustration.
- **Universal Design Integration:** AI that automatically generates accessible versions of all materials—braille, captions, simplified text.
- **Contextual Adaptation:** AI that recognizes cultural and linguistic contexts, ensuring inclusivity across diverse classrooms.
- **Wearable AI:** Devices that provide real-time translation, captioning, or text-to-speech support in classrooms.

These innovations point to a future where inclusion is not an add-on but built into the fabric of education.

Key Takeaway

AI offers unprecedented opportunities to make education inclusive for all learners. From captioning lectures for hearing-impaired students to adaptive reading tools for dyslexia, AI removes barriers and personalizes support at scale.

Yet inclusion is not automatic. Without ethical oversight, AI may reinforce bias, invade privacy, or widen divides. The challenge is to ensure AI is designed and implemented with inclusivity at its core.

When done responsibly, AI can transform classrooms into spaces where every student—regardless of ability, language, or background—has the tools they need to learn, participate, and succeed.

CHAPTER 4

Data, Analytics, and Assessment

Learning Analytics Explained

For centuries, teachers have relied on observation, instinct, and occasional test scores to understand how students learn. These methods, while valuable, are limited in scope and often retrospective: educators know how a student performed only after the fact. In today's digital classrooms, however, every click, keystroke, and interaction generates data. The field of **learning analytics** harnesses this data to reveal insights about how students learn, where they struggle, and what can be done to support them more effectively.

Artificial Intelligence takes learning analytics further. Instead of simply collecting and presenting data, AI interprets patterns, predicts outcomes, and offers actionable recommendations. For teachers, this means moving from reactive to proactive decision-making. For students, it means receiving more personalized and timely support.

What Is Learning Analytics?

At its simplest, learning analytics is the measurement, collection, and analysis of data about learners and their contexts, with the goal of improving learning. Examples include:

- Tracking how long a student spends on an assignment.
- Measuring which concepts generate the most mistakes.
- Analyzing participation in online discussions.
- Mapping overall course engagement trends.

These insights help educators and institutions make informed decisions about instruction, curriculum, and support services.

But AI transforms analytics from static dashboards into **dynamic intelligence systems** that learn from data, adapt over time, and generate predictions.

The Traditional Approach to Analytics

Before AI integration, learning analytics often looked like spreadsheets or graphs showing attendance, grades, or participation rates. These tools were helpful but descriptive: they told educators *what happened* but not *why* it happened or *what to do next*.

For example, a teacher might see that half the class failed a quiz. Traditional analytics would display the scores, perhaps even highlighting the most-missed questions. But it would not explain why students struggled, nor suggest tailored interventions.

AI-enhanced learning analytics changes this by moving from description to **diagnosis and prediction**.

How AI Transforms Learning Analytics

AI makes analytics more powerful in four key ways:

1. **Pattern Recognition:** AI can detect subtle trends invisible to the human eye. For instance, it might identify that students who pause frequently before answering tend to struggle later in the course.
2. **Prediction:** By analyzing historical data, AI predicts future outcomes—such as which students are at risk of dropping out or which topics will cause difficulty.
3. **Personalization:** AI tailors recommendations for each learner, suggesting practice activities, resources, or pacing adjustments.
4. **Real-Time Adaptation:** Instead of waiting until the end of a unit, AI can highlight challenges as they occur, enabling immediate intervention.

This shifts analytics from being a rear-view mirror to a GPS system guiding learning in real time.

Case Study 1: Purdue University's Course Signals

Purdue University was an early pioneer in AI-powered learning analytics with its **Course Signals** system. The platform used student data—grades, attendance, online activity—to predict academic risk. Students were flagged with a "traffic light" system: green for on track, yellow for caution, red for high risk.

Faculty could then reach out proactively to struggling students. Studies showed that students flagged early were more likely to seek help, leading to higher retention and success rates.

Case Study 2: Georgia State University

Georgia State implemented predictive analytics to identify students at risk of dropping out. The system tracked over **800 risk factors**, from course selection to GPA patterns. When risks were flagged, advisors intervened with targeted support.

The results were striking: graduation rates rose significantly, particularly for first-generation and minority students. AI analytics helped close equity gaps by ensuring no student "fell through the cracks" unnoticed.

Case Study 3: K–12 Adaptive Dashboards

In K–12 schools, AI dashboards are increasingly used to monitor student engagement. For example, DreamBox Learning provides teachers with real-time reports on how students interact with math content. If a student repeatedly struggles with fractions, the dashboard highlights this immediately, allowing teachers to adjust instruction before the issue snowballs.

Benefits for Students

AI-driven learning analytics offers significant advantages for learners:

- **Timely Support:** Struggling students are identified early, preventing failure.
- **Personalized Recommendations:** Students receive resources tailored to their specific gaps.
- **Increased Self-Awareness:** Dashboards help students monitor their own progress, building metacognitive skills.
- **Equity in Support:** Analytics can highlight systemic inequities, ensuring interventions reach underserved groups.

Students who might otherwise feel invisible in large classes gain visibility through data-driven insights.

Benefits for Teachers

For educators, learning analytics powered by AI provides:

- **Targeted Interventions:** Instead of relying on intuition, teachers see exactly which students need what kind of help.
- **Instructional Insights:** Teachers learn which lessons are most effective and which need revision.
- **Time Efficiency:** Data analysis that once took hours is automated, freeing teachers to focus on students.
- **Professional Growth:** Analytics highlight areas where teachers themselves can improve instructional strategies.

A teacher described analytics as “a second pair of eyes”—constantly monitoring and surfacing insights that no human could track alone.

Institutional Impact

At the school and university level, AI analytics informs:

- **Curriculum Design:** Identifying which courses or modules consistently cause difficulties.
- **Resource Allocation:** Directing tutoring or support services where they are most needed.
- **Policy Decisions:** Understanding equity gaps, student progression, and overall institutional performance.

Institutions using AI analytics often see improved retention rates, higher student satisfaction, and more efficient use of resources.

Risks and Challenges

Despite its potential, learning analytics comes with risks:

1. **Privacy Concerns:** Collecting detailed data on student behavior raises questions about consent, storage, and ownership.
2. **Surveillance Anxiety:** Students may feel over-monitored, leading to stress or resistance.
3. **Algorithmic Bias:** If models are trained on biased data, predictions may unfairly disadvantage certain groups.
4. **Over-Reliance on Data:** Reducing learners to numbers risks ignoring creativity, critical thinking, and socio-emotional growth.

One of the greatest dangers is **labeling**: if an AI system predicts a student is "at risk," teachers or advisors may lower expectations, inadvertently limiting opportunities.

Ethical Considerations

Ethical implementation of learning analytics requires:

- **Transparency:** Students and teachers must understand what data is collected and how it is used.
- **Consent:** Learners should have agency over their own data.
- **Equity Audits:** Regular checks to ensure analytics serve all students fairly.
- **Human Oversight:** Teachers and advisors, not algorithms alone, must interpret data and make decisions.

The goal is not to replace human judgment but to enrich it with evidence-based insights.

The Future of Learning Analytics

AI will continue to evolve learning analytics in several directions:

- **Emotion and Engagement Tracking:** Using facial and voice recognition to detect frustration or boredom in real time.
- **Holistic Analytics:** Integrating academic, social, and well-being data to support the whole student.
- **Predictive Pathways:** Suggesting career and life paths based on patterns in student interests and achievements.
- **Cross-Institutional Analytics:** Sharing anonymized data across schools and universities to identify broader educational trends.

These innovations must be pursued carefully, ensuring that analytics empowers learners rather than reducing them to data points.

Key Takeaway

Learning analytics, supercharged by AI, transforms raw data into actionable insights that improve teaching, personalize learning, and guide institutional strategy. When used responsibly, it enables earlier interventions, stronger equity, and more effective education systems.

But analytics is not neutral. Without transparency, ethical safeguards, and human oversight, it risks becoming surveillance or reinforcing inequities. Done thoughtfully, learning analytics ensures that no learner is invisible—and that every student's journey is seen, supported, and valued.

Predictive Analytics for Success

Education has always involved prediction. Teachers estimate how well a student might do on an exam, counselors forecast whether a student is ready for college, and administrators anticipate graduation rates. But these predictions have traditionally been based on intuition, limited data, or broad averages. Artificial Intelligence now makes it possible to predict educational outcomes with far greater precision, using vast amounts of data to forecast student success—and intervene before problems become crises.

Predictive analytics does not just describe what *has* happened; it forecasts what *is likely* to happen. For schools, this shift from hindsight to foresight is transformative. It enables proactive support, targeted interventions, and systemic improvements that increase equity and achievement.

What Is Predictive Analytics?

Predictive analytics is the use of data, statistical models, and machine learning to identify the likelihood of future outcomes. In education, it often answers questions like:

- Which students are at risk of dropping out?

- Who is likely to fail a course without intervention?
- What learning paths are most effective for specific groups of students?
- How can institutions allocate resources to maximize student success?

By analyzing patterns across thousands—or even millions—of learners, AI-powered predictive models reveal insights far beyond human capacity.

The Promise of Early Intervention

One of the most powerful applications of predictive analytics is early intervention. Instead of discovering failure at the end of a semester, schools can identify risks in real time and act immediately.

For example:

- A high school notices that a student's attendance has declined and their homework completion rate has dropped. Predictive analytics combines these signals with historical patterns to forecast a high risk of course failure. The teacher is alerted, allowing intervention through tutoring, counseling, or parent engagement.
- A university tracks course performance across majors. The system predicts that students who receive below a C in introductory math are unlikely to complete engineering programs. Advisors can guide struggling students toward support services before they fall behind.

This ability to "see around corners" can dramatically change student trajectories.

Case Study 1: Georgia State University

Georgia State University (GSU) is one of the most celebrated examples of predictive analytics in action. Using AI-driven systems, GSU monitors over **800 variables per student**—including grades, course choices, attendance, and registration patterns. When risk factors are detected, advisors receive alerts to reach out proactively.

The results are remarkable:

- Graduation rates increased by more than 20 percentage points over a decade.
- Achievement gaps between white and minority students narrowed significantly.
- Thousands of students avoided dropping out thanks to timely interventions.

GSU demonstrates how predictive analytics, when paired with human support, can transform institutional outcomes.

Case Study 2: Rio Salado College

Rio Salado College, an online institution in Arizona, uses predictive analytics to identify struggling students early in virtual courses. Algorithms track login frequency, assignment submissions, and quiz performance. If patterns indicate a risk of dropout, advisors contact the student within 48 hours.

This rapid-response model has been shown to improve retention, especially among adult learners balancing education with work and family responsibilities.

Case Study 3: K–12 Predictive Models

In K–12 settings, predictive analytics is used to identify students at risk of not meeting grade-level standards. For example, some districts use AI to analyze reading fluency data from early grades. By predicting which students may struggle later, schools can provide targeted literacy interventions in elementary years—preventing long-term academic struggles.

Benefits for Students

Predictive analytics benefits learners in several ways:

- **Personalized Support:** At-risk students receive interventions tailored to their needs before failure occurs.
- **Equity Gains:** Analytics highlight disparities, ensuring underserved students are not overlooked.
- **Improved Confidence:** Timely support prevents discouragement, keeping students engaged.
- **Pathway Guidance:** Students receive recommendations about courses, majors, or careers aligned with their strengths.

For students who might otherwise "fall through the cracks," predictive models act as a safety net.

Benefits for Teachers and Advisors

Educators also gain critical advantages:

- **Actionable Insights:** Teachers no longer rely solely on intuition to identify struggling students.
- **Efficiency:** Advisors focus on students who most need help, rather than spreading efforts thinly.
- **Better Outcomes:** Predictive models improve success rates, reflecting positively on both teachers and institutions.

A teacher once described predictive analytics as "a radar system"—constantly scanning for risks so interventions are timely rather than reactive.

Benefits for Institutions

At the institutional level, predictive analytics guides strategic decision-making:

- **Resource Allocation:** Schools can direct tutoring, counseling, and financial aid to students most likely to benefit.
- **Retention and Graduation Rates:** Institutions improve performance metrics that affect funding and reputation.
- **Program Evaluation:** Analytics reveal which courses or teaching methods consistently lead to success—or failure.

For universities facing pressure to improve retention, predictive analytics is becoming a cornerstone strategy.

Risks and Challenges

Despite its promise, predictive analytics raises serious concerns:

1. **Bias in Predictions:** If historical data reflects inequalities, AI may reinforce them. For example, if students from low-income backgrounds have historically lower graduation rates, models may "predict" failure unfairly.
2. **Labeling Students:** Being flagged as "at risk" may stigmatize students or lower expectations from teachers.
3. **Privacy Issues:** Continuous monitoring requires sensitive student data, raising ethical concerns about ownership and security.
4. **Over-Reliance on Data:** Predictions should guide, not dictate. Human judgment must remain central.

Without safeguards, predictive analytics can harm the very students it aims to support.

Ethical Implementation

To use predictive analytics responsibly, schools should:

- **Be Transparent:** Students must understand what data is collected and how predictions are used.
- **Ensure Human Oversight:** Teachers and advisors—not algorithms—should make final decisions.
- **Audit for Bias:** Models must be tested regularly to prevent inequitable predictions.
- **Avoid Determinism:** Predictions should be seen as risk indicators, not fixed destinies.

An ethical mantra might be: *Predict to support, not to sort.*

Global Trends

- **United States:** Widespread adoption in higher education, with many universities building predictive systems for retention.
- **Europe:** Cautious adoption due to stronger privacy laws, emphasizing consent and data protection.
- **Asia:** Countries like Singapore and China integrate predictive analytics into national education strategies, though concerns about surveillance persist.
- **Africa:** Emerging initiatives use predictive models to improve literacy and reduce dropout in resource-constrained schools.

Global diversity in implementation reflects cultural and policy differences in balancing innovation with ethics.

The Future of Predictive Analytics

Looking ahead, predictive systems may expand in several directions:

- **Real-Time Risk Detection:** Identifying disengagement within minutes, not weeks.
- **Holistic Predictions:** Integrating academic, behavioral, and socio-emotional data for more accurate forecasts.
- **Career Pathway Guidance:** Using long-term data to suggest career options aligned with strengths and interests.
- **AI Advisors:** Automated systems providing recommendations directly to students, paired with human support.

The challenge will be ensuring these systems empower learners rather than reducing them to probabilities.

Key Takeaway

Predictive analytics is one of AI's most powerful tools in education. By forecasting risks and opportunities, it enables earlier interventions, higher success rates, and more equitable outcomes. For students, it provides timely support. For teachers, it offers actionable insights. For institutions, it drives systemic improvement.

But predictive power must be handled with care. Without ethical safeguards, it risks bias, surveillance, or deterministic labeling. The goal is not to predict failure but to prevent it—using data not as a sentence but as a guide toward growth and opportunity.

AI-Powered Assessment Systems

Assessment has always been a cornerstone of education. It tells teachers how well students have learned, guides decisions about progression, and provides feedback to learners themselves. Yet, traditional assessment methods—standardized tests, multiple-choice exams, essays—are often rigid, time-consuming, and limited in scope. They frequently measure only what is easy to test, not what truly matters.

Artificial Intelligence is reshaping assessment. By automating grading, analyzing open-ended responses, and providing real-time feedback, AI-powered systems expand what can be assessed, how it is assessed, and how quickly results reach students and teachers. The promise is clear: more efficient, fairer, and more meaningful assessments that align with the complexity of learning in the modern world.

The Limits of Traditional Assessment

Traditional assessment methods have well-documented shortcomings:

- **Time Burden:** Teachers spend countless hours grading essays, projects, and tests.
- **Delayed Feedback:** By the time students receive results, the moment for effective correction may have passed.
- **Narrow Focus:** Standardized tests often prioritize rote memorization over critical thinking, creativity, or problem-solving.
- **Subjectivity:** Grading essays or projects can be inconsistent, with outcomes influenced by teacher bias, fatigue, or mood.
- **One-Size-Fits-All:** Standardized assessments do not account for diverse learning styles, backgrounds, or needs.

AI-powered systems aim to address these challenges by making assessment more **adaptive, scalable, and precise**.

What AI Brings to Assessment

AI transforms assessment in several key ways:

1. **Automated Grading:** AI can evaluate essays, short answers, and even creative work by analyzing structure, coherence, and originality.

2. **Real-Time Feedback:** Students receive immediate insights, allowing them to correct mistakes before they become habits.
3. **Adaptive Testing:** AI adjusts question difficulty in real time based on responses, ensuring assessments accurately reflect ability levels.
4. **Deeper Analysis:** Beyond right and wrong, AI can analyze reasoning patterns, creativity, and problem-solving strategies.
5. **Scalability:** Large classes or online programs can provide individualized feedback at scale.

These shifts reframe assessment as an ongoing learning process rather than a one-time judgment.

Case Study 1: Gradescope

Gradescope, used widely in universities, leverages AI to streamline grading. Teachers upload student work, and AI helps group similar answers, allowing faster and more consistent grading. In large STEM courses, professors have reported cutting grading time in half. Importantly, AI does not replace human judgment but assists it, ensuring greater efficiency without sacrificing fairness.

Case Study 2: Turnitin

Turnitin, initially known for plagiarism detection, now uses AI to evaluate writing quality. Its tools analyze grammar, clarity, and originality while also offering feedback on argumentation and structure. Students receive formative feedback before final submission, turning assessment into a cycle of growth rather than a one-time penalty.

Case Study 3: Pearson's AI Assessments

Pearson, a global education company, has piloted AI-driven assessments that adapt in real time. If a student answers correctly, the system offers harder questions; if incorrectly, easier ones. This adaptive model creates a more accurate profile of ability than static multiple-choice tests.

Benefits for Students

AI-powered assessments provide significant advantages:

- **Instant Feedback:** Students know immediately where they went wrong and how to improve.
- **Personalized Learning:** Adaptive tests meet learners at their level, reducing frustration and boredom.
- **Confidence Building:** Frequent, low-stakes assessments encourage growth rather than fear of failure.
- **Equity Gains:** AI can reduce human bias, offering consistent evaluation across diverse students.

For example, a student practicing essay writing can submit drafts to an AI system multiple times, receiving guidance before the teacher reviews the final version. This iterative process promotes learning rather than punishment.

Benefits for Teachers

Teachers also benefit:

- **Time Savings:** Automated grading reduces workload, freeing teachers for mentoring and instruction.
- **Consistency:** AI applies rubrics uniformly, minimizing subjective variation.
- **Diagnostic Insights:** AI highlights common misconceptions across a class, informing targeted re-teaching.
- **Enhanced Feedback:** Teachers can focus feedback on higher-order thinking while AI handles mechanics

One university professor explained: *"AI doesn't grade for me—it prepares the ground. I can focus my comments on critical thinking instead of grammar errors."*

Institutional Benefits

At the institutional level, AI-powered assessment supports:

- **Scalability:** Online courses with thousands of students can still provide individualized feedback.
- **Data-Driven Decisions:** Institutions can analyze assessment data to evaluate program effectiveness.
- **Cost Efficiency:** Automated systems reduce the expense of manual grading in large-scale education.

This scalability is especially critical for MOOCs (Massive Open Online Courses), where traditional grading is impossible at scale.

Risks and Challenges

Despite the promise, AI assessment systems raise concerns:

1. **Bias and Fairness:** AI models may undervalue non-standard writing styles, cultural references, or creative approaches.
2. **Accuracy Issues:** Generative AI sometimes provides incorrect feedback, requiring oversight.
3. **Over-Standardization:** Reliance on algorithms risks narrowing definitions of "good" writing or problem-solving.
4. **Privacy Concerns:** Storing student work raises questions about ownership and data security.
5. **Reduced Human Connection:** If students only receive AI feedback, they may feel disconnected from their teachers.

These risks highlight that AI should assist, not replace, human assessment.

Ethical Considerations

To implement AI-powered assessments ethically, schools should:

- **Maintain Human Oversight:** Teachers must review and validate AI-generated feedback.
- **Ensure Transparency:** Students should understand how their work is being evaluated.
- **Protect Creativity:** Systems must allow for originality rather than rewarding conformity.
- **Prioritize Privacy:** Student work must be stored and managed securely.

The principle should be: AI enhances fairness and efficiency but does not define learning on its own.

The Future of AI Assessment

Looking ahead, AI-powered assessment may expand into new frontiers:

- **Multi-Modal Assessment:** Evaluating not just text or numbers but also speech, presentations, art, and collaboration.
- **Emotion-Aware Feedback:** Detecting stress or frustration during tests and offering encouragement.
- **Portfolio-Based Assessment:** AI curating long-term collections of student work to reflect holistic growth.
- **Authentic Learning Evaluation:** Assessing problem-solving in real-world simulations rather than abstract tests.

The future of assessment is not just faster grading but richer, more human-centered evaluation.

Key Takeaway

AI-powered assessment systems reimagine how learning is measured. They provide instant feedback, adaptive testing, and scalable evaluation that benefits students, teachers, and institutions alike.

But technology alone cannot define success. Without oversight, AI risks bias, conformity, and detachment from the human side of education. The opportunity lies in combining AI's efficiency with teachers' empathy and judgment, ensuring assessment becomes not just a tool of measurement, but a driver of learning and growth.

Balancing Data Privacy and Innovation

Artificial Intelligence thrives on data. The more information systems have about student performance, behavior, and engagement, the more accurately they can personalize learning, predict outcomes, and support teachers. Yet this dependence on data creates one of education's greatest ethical challenges: how to innovate with AI while protecting the privacy, dignity, and rights of learners.

In education, data is not abstract—it represents children and young people at formative stages of life. Mishandling this information can have profound consequences, from loss of trust to long-term harm. The challenge is not whether to use data, but how to use it responsibly, ensuring that innovation enhances, rather than endangers, students' futures.

The Nature of Student Data

Student data goes far beyond test scores. In AI-powered education, it may include:

- Demographics (age, gender, socioeconomic background).
- Academic records (grades, assignments, attendance).
- Behavioral patterns (time on tasks, logins, participation).

- Biometric data (voice, facial recognition, eye-tracking in some systems).
- Emotional cues (tone of voice, engagement indicators).

This creates a rich but sensitive portrait of learners. Unlike adults who choose to share personal information, students often have little agency in how their data is collected or used. This asymmetry of power makes privacy in education especially urgent.

The Promise of Data in Education

Used responsibly, student data enables remarkable innovations:

- **Personalized Learning:** AI tailors instruction to individual strengths and weaknesses.
- **Early Intervention:** At-risk students are identified before failure occurs.
- **Institutional Insights:** Schools gain data to allocate resources effectively.
- **Equity Monitoring:** Analytics reveal systemic disparities, guiding policy change.

Without data, these advances would be impossible. The goal is not to restrict innovation, but to balance it with protections that preserve trust and fairness.

The Risks of Data Misuse

The risks of educational data misuse are significant:

1. **Commercial Exploitation:** Some EdTech companies collect student data for advertising or resale, raising serious ethical concerns.
2. **Security Breaches:** Student databases are vulnerable to hacking, exposing sensitive information.
3. **Permanent Records:** Data collected in childhood may follow students indefinitely, affecting future opportunities.

4. **Surveillance Culture:** Excessive monitoring can create environments of mistrust, discouraging risk-taking and creativity.
5. **Algorithmic Bias:** Data-driven systems may reinforce inequalities if not carefully audited.

A single data breach or misuse can erode trust not only in one platform, but in AI adoption across entire systems.

Case Study 1: The Proctoring Controversy

During the COVID-19 pandemic, many universities adopted AI-powered remote proctoring tools to monitor students during exams. These systems collected biometric data through webcams, tracked eye movements, and flagged "suspicious behavior."

While intended to ensure fairness, they sparked backlash. Students reported anxiety, privacy violations, and false accusations. Facial recognition algorithms sometimes failed to recognize students with darker skin tones, compounding inequities. This case illustrates how innovation without adequate safeguards can undermine trust and harm learners.

Case Study 2: Google's Education Tools

In 2020, Google faced lawsuits alleging it collected biometric data from students using its education platforms without consent. The controversy raised questions about whether companies providing free educational tools were profiting from sensitive student information.

This example highlights the blurred line between innovation and exploitation when corporate interests intersect with public education.

Regulations and Frameworks

Different regions approach privacy differently:

- **European Union:** The **General Data Protection Regulation (GDPR)** gives individuals strong rights over their data, including students. Schools must ensure informed consent and data minimization.
- **United States:** Laws like **FERPA (Family Educational Rights and Privacy Act)** and **COPPA (Children's Online Privacy Protection Act)** regulate student data, but enforcement is fragmented and often outdated.
- **Asia:** Countries like Singapore emphasize strong data governance frameworks, while China has looser protections, raising concerns about surveillance in education.

These regulations set important boundaries but must adapt continually to keep pace with AI's capabilities.

Strategies for Balancing Privacy and Innovation

1. **Data Minimization**
   Collect only what is necessary. If a reading app can function without storing geolocation, it should not collect it. Minimization reduces both risks and ethical concerns.
2. **Transparency and Consent**
   Students and parents must understand what data is collected, why, and how it will be used. Consent should be informed, not buried in long legal documents.
3. **Student Agency**
   Where possible, students should have control over their data, including the ability to view, correct, or delete records. Empowering learners builds trust.
4. **Anonymization**
   When data is used for research or institutional analysis, it should be anonymized to prevent individual identification.

5. **Security Protocols**
   Strong encryption, secure storage, and regular audits are essential to protect data against breaches.
6. **Ethical Audits**
   Independent audits should evaluate whether AI systems are fair, unbiased, and respectful of privacy.

The Role of Teachers and Institutions

Teachers play a crucial role in mediating data use. They must understand how AI systems collect and analyze information and advocate for their students' rights. Institutions must develop clear policies that prioritize learning over commercial interests.

Training teachers in **data literacy** is key: they should be able to explain to students how their data is used and make informed decisions about which tools to adopt.

Students' Right to Privacy

Students are not simply data points—they are individuals with rights. Balancing innovation with privacy means treating data as a form of trust. Collecting it obligates schools and companies to use it ethically and protect it rigorously.

As one student advocacy group put it: *"We are not customers; we are learners. Our data should not be currency."*

Future Directions in Privacy-Conscious Innovation

Looking ahead, balancing privacy and innovation will involve:

- **Privacy by Design:** Building systems with privacy protections integrated from the start, not as add-ons.
- **Federated Learning:** AI models trained on decentralized data, reducing the need for central storage.

- **Student Data Portfolios:** Systems where students own and manage their own learning data, choosing what to share.
- **Global Standards:** International frameworks ensuring consistent protections across borders.

These innovations suggest a future where data privacy and AI advancement are not in conflict but aligned.

Key Takeaway

AI-driven education depends on data, but data must never come at the cost of student rights. Balancing privacy and innovation requires transparency, consent, and safeguards that respect learners as individuals, not commodities.

Handled responsibly, data becomes a tool of empowerment—fueling personalization, equity, and growth. Mishandled, it becomes a source of mistrust and harm. The path forward is clear: build systems where innovation and privacy reinforce each other, ensuring that AI serves learners without compromising their dignity.

CHAPTER 5

AI for Administrative and Institutional Support

Automating Administrative Tasks

Behind every classroom lesson lies a world of administration. From scheduling and attendance to enrollment and record-keeping, schools and universities spend enormous amounts of time and resources managing logistics. These tasks are essential for institutions to function, but they consume hours of effort that could otherwise be devoted to teaching and learning.

Artificial Intelligence offers a powerful solution: the automation of routine administrative processes. By handling repetitive and time-intensive tasks, AI enables schools to operate more efficiently, reduce costs, and free educators to focus on their primary mission—supporting students.

The Administrative Burden in Education

To appreciate the potential of AI, it helps to understand the scale of the problem. In the United States, a 2019 study found that teachers spend nearly **seven hours per week** on administrative work—time taken away from lesson preparation and student interaction. School administrators face even greater loads, juggling student records, compliance reporting, financial management, and communication with families.

Universities are no different. Registrar offices manage thousands of student records, admissions departments process applications at scale, and faculty spend hours navigating complex systems for scheduling and grading.

This administrative load leads to:

- **Burnout:** Teachers and administrators overwhelmed by paperwork.
- **Inefficiency:** Delays in communication and decision-making.
- **Cost:** Resources spent on administration rather than instruction.

AI automation offers relief by taking on these repetitive tasks with speed, accuracy, and consistency.

Key Areas of Automation

1. **Attendance and Record-Keeping**
   Traditionally, teachers take attendance manually, a process prone to errors and time-wasting. AI systems can automate this through digital check-ins, biometric systems, or facial recognition (when ethically implemented). Attendance is logged instantly, with data synced to school records.
2. **Scheduling**
   Creating timetables for hundreds—or thousands—of students and staff is a logistical nightmare. AI scheduling tools analyze constraints (room availability, teacher preferences, student course selections) and generate optimal timetables in minutes. They can also adjust dynamically if a teacher is absent or a class size changes.
3. **Admissions and Enrollment**
   Universities receive tens of thousands of applications each year. AI can scan applications, categorize candidates, and flag those meeting specific criteria. While final decisions remain human, automation streamlines the initial review process. In K–12, AI systems simplify enrollment by managing forms, verifying eligibility, and assigning placements.
4. **Communication**
   AI-powered chatbots are increasingly used to answer routine questions from students and parents. Instead of administrators fielding thousands of emails about deadlines or policies, chatbots provide instant responses. Some universities report that chatbots resolve up to **80% of inquiries** without human intervention.
5. **Grading and Data Entry**
   While grading overlaps with assessment, administrative data entry—such as uploading grades, updating transcripts, or reporting compliance data—can be automated. AI ensures accuracy and reduces the risk of clerical errors.

Case Study 1: Georgia State University's Pounce Chatbot

Georgia State introduced an AI chatbot named **Pounce** to handle student questions during the admissions process. Many students, especially first-generation college applicants, fail to enroll because they miss deadlines or misunderstand forms—a phenomenon known as "summer melt."

Pounce answered thousands of questions via text, guiding students through the process. The result: a **22% reduction in summer melt**, demonstrating how simple administrative automation can have life-changing outcomes for students.

Case Study 2: AI Scheduling in Indian Schools

In India, large urban schools often struggle with complex timetabling for thousands of students. AI-powered scheduling systems have been piloted to optimize teacher assignments, room usage, and class sizes. Schools report significant reductions in scheduling errors and improved teacher satisfaction, as preferences and workload balance are better accounted for.

Case Study 3: Chatbots in UK Universities

Several UK universities have deployed AI chatbots to manage student services. These bots answer questions about housing, financial aid, course registration, and campus events. Surveys show students appreciate 24/7 availability, while administrators save hundreds of hours each term.

Benefits for Teachers

For educators, administrative automation means:

- **More Time for Teaching:** Less paperwork, more focus on students.

- **Reduced Stress:** Freed from repetitive tasks, teachers experience less burnout.
- **Improved Accuracy:** Automated systems reduce human error in records and reporting.

One teacher described AI attendance tools as "a small miracle"—removing the daily ritual of roll call and giving back valuable instructional time.

Benefits for Institutions

At the school or university level, automation delivers:

- **Efficiency Gains:** Faster processes for enrollment, scheduling, and communication.
- **Cost Savings:** Reduced administrative overhead.
- **Better Decision-Making:** Accurate, up-to-date records inform policy and planning.
- **Improved Student Experience:** Faster responses and smoother processes enhance satisfaction.

Institutions that adopt AI automation often see both operational improvements and reputational gains, as students and families experience more streamlined services.

Risks and Challenges

While automation offers efficiency, it also raises concerns:

1. **Privacy:** Systems like facial recognition for attendance risk misuse of biometric data.
2. **Equity:** Schools with fewer resources may lack access to advanced automation, widening institutional divides.
3. **Job Displacement:** Administrative staff may fear replacement, requiring careful planning and reskilling.
4. **Over-Reliance:** Excessive dependence on AI may reduce flexibility or human judgment in exceptional cases.

Balancing efficiency with ethics is critical to ensure automation serves people rather than replacing them.

Ethical Implementation

To implement automation responsibly, schools should:

- **Maintain Human Oversight:** Critical decisions (admissions, placements) should remain human-led.
- **Ensure Transparency:** Families must understand how their data is collected and used.
- **Prioritize Security:** Automated systems should adhere to strict data protection standards.
- **Support Staff Transition:** Provide training so administrative staff can move into higher-value roles rather than being displaced.

The goal is not to eliminate human workers but to elevate their roles by removing repetitive burdens.

The Future of Administrative Automation

Looking forward, automation may expand into:

- **Predictive Scheduling:** Systems anticipating resource needs months in advance.
- **Voice-Activated Administration:** Teachers managing records through simple voice commands.
- **Integrated Platforms:** Seamless AI systems uniting attendance, grading, communication, and scheduling into one ecosystem.
- **Smart Resource Management:** AI predicting supply needs (books, lab materials) based on enrollment trends.

The future of administration is not just efficiency—it is intelligence, where schools operate like well-tuned systems that anticipate needs and adjust in real time.

Key Takeaway

AI-powered automation of administrative tasks represents one of the clearest and least controversial benefits of AI in education. By handling attendance, scheduling, enrollment, and communication, AI saves time, reduces errors, and enhances both teacher and student experiences.

The risks—privacy, equity, job displacement—are real but manageable with ethical frameworks and human oversight. Done thoughtfully, administrative automation ensures education systems function smoothly, freeing teachers and administrators to do what technology cannot: nurture, inspire, and lead human growth.

AI in Resource Allocation

Education is not just about classrooms and lessons—it is also about resources. Schools and universities must decide how to distribute budgets, assign teachers, manage facilities, and support programs. These choices are complex, often political, and carry high stakes: the way resources are allocated can directly impact the quality of education students receive.

Artificial Intelligence offers new tools to support resource allocation. By analyzing data, forecasting needs, and suggesting optimal distribution strategies, AI can help institutions stretch limited budgets further, reduce waste, and ensure fairness. Yet as with all AI in education, resource allocation raises ethical questions: Who benefits from AI-driven decisions? Who might be left behind? And how do schools balance efficiency with equity?

The Resource Challenge in Education

Resource allocation has always been difficult because educational needs are vast while resources are limited. Consider the following challenges:

- **Budget Constraints:** Many schools operate under tight budgets, forced to choose between updating technology, hiring staff, or maintaining facilities.
- **Teacher Shortages:** Some subjects (such as STEM or special education) face chronic shortages, making staffing decisions critical.
- **Infrastructure Needs:** Schools must balance investment in buildings, labs, libraries, and digital tools.
- **Equity Demands:** Institutions must ensure resources reach underserved communities and students with additional needs.

Traditionally, these decisions are made through human judgment, political negotiation, or historical precedent. AI introduces a new layer: data-driven insights that can guide choices with greater accuracy.

How AI Supports Resource Allocation

AI contributes to smarter allocation in several key ways:

1. **Budget Optimization**
   AI systems can analyze financial data and forecast the long-term impact of different spending choices. For example, they might compare the outcomes of investing in new laptops versus hiring additional support staff, showing which option would improve student success more effectively.
2. **Staffing and Scheduling**
   AI tools predict teacher demand based on enrollment trends, retirements, and subject-specific shortages. They can also optimize scheduling to balance workloads and reduce burnout.
3. **Facilities Management**
   AI can monitor energy use, building occupancy, and maintenance needs, allowing schools to save money and plan upgrades strategically. For example, predictive maintenance systems alert administrators before equipment fails, reducing costly emergencies.

4. **Student Support Services**
   Resource allocation is not just about money—it's also about attention. AI identifies which students require tutoring, counseling, or financial aid, ensuring support is directed to those most in need.
5. **Long-Term Forecasting**
   By analyzing demographic trends, AI predicts future enrollment and resource needs, allowing schools to plan years in advance.

Case Study 1: Los Angeles Unified School District

The **Los Angeles Unified School District (LAUSD)** has experimented with AI-driven analytics to guide staffing and resource allocation. By predicting enrollment shifts, the system helps administrators determine where new teachers are needed most. This reduces mismatches—such as overstaffing in one school while another struggles with shortages.

Case Study 2: Arizona State University

Arizona State uses AI to forecast classroom and facility needs. By tracking course enrollments, the university can anticipate demand for lecture halls, labs, or online resources. This ensures infrastructure investments match actual student use, preventing waste.

Case Study 3: Rural Schools in India

In rural India, AI systems have been used to allocate scarce resources such as textbooks and laptops. By analyzing school attendance and performance data, NGOs identify which schools will benefit most from specific resources. This targeted distribution improves efficiency and reduces inequality.

Benefits for Students

AI-driven resource allocation improves student experiences by:

- **Ensuring Equity:** Resources are distributed based on need rather than politics or tradition.
- **Reducing Shortages:** Predictive staffing ensures students are less likely to face empty classrooms or canceled courses.
- **Enhancing Learning Environments:** Smarter facility management creates safer, better-equipped classrooms.
- **Targeted Support:** At-risk students receive interventions like tutoring or counseling when they need them most.

For example, if predictive analytics show a rise in mental health concerns among students, schools can allocate more counselors rather than waiting for a crisis.

Benefits for Teachers

Teachers also gain from better allocation:

- **Balanced Workloads:** AI ensures staffing and scheduling are distributed fairly.
- **Improved Resources:** Teachers receive the technology and materials they need more reliably.
- **Reduced Stress:** With adequate support services, teachers can focus on instruction rather than compensating for resource gaps.

One teacher described AI-driven scheduling as "the first time my workload felt fair compared to colleagues in other departments."

Institutional Benefits

At the institutional level, AI resource allocation offers:

- **Cost Efficiency:** Smarter budgeting reduces waste.
- **Transparency:** Data-driven decisions reduce accusations of favoritism or bias.
- **Long-Term Planning:** AI forecasts allow for proactive investment in staff, facilities, and technology.
- **Reputation:** Schools that manage resources well attract students and retain staff.

These gains make resource allocation one of AI's most practical applications in education.

Risks and Concerns

Yet there are significant risks:

1. **Equity Blind Spots**
   AI may optimize for efficiency at the expense of equity. For example, it might allocate resources to schools where investment yields the "highest return" rather than to those serving marginalized communities.
2. **Data Limitations**
   If data is incomplete or biased, resource decisions may reinforce existing inequalities.
3. **Job Displacement**
   Automation in facilities or administrative tasks may reduce the need for certain staff roles.
4. **Over-Dependence**
   Leaders may rely too heavily on AI recommendations, reducing human judgment and flexibility in decision-making.

Ethical Resource Allocation

To ensure fairness, schools must adopt principles of ethical allocation:

- **Equity First:** Prioritize resources for underserved communities, even if less "efficient" on paper.
- **Transparency:** Explain how AI makes recommendations and involve stakeholders in decisions.
- **Human Oversight:** Final allocation decisions should rest with people, not machines.
- **Inclusive Data:** Ensure datasets reflect diverse contexts and communities.

AI should be a tool for justice, not just efficiency.

The Global Outlook

- **United States:** Universities and districts use AI to manage budgets and staffing but face pushback around transparency.
- **Europe:** Stronger regulations emphasize fairness in allocation, especially in public schools.
- **China:** Large-scale AI systems optimize resource use nationwide, though concerns about surveillance persist.
- **Developing Countries:** AI is often used to maximize scarce resources, such as textbooks or teacher time, in underserved regions.

The global landscape shows that AI's impact depends heavily on values: whether institutions prioritize efficiency, equity, or both.

The Future of Resource Allocation

In the future, AI may expand into:

- **Dynamic Resource Management:** Real-time reallocation of resources as needs shift daily.

- **Integrated Ecosystems:** AI systems linking budgets, staffing, and student data for holistic decision-making.
- **Sustainability Optimization:** AI guiding investments in green infrastructure to reduce environmental impact.
- **Participatory Models:** Students, teachers, and communities influencing AI resource decisions through democratic input.

The ultimate vision is not just smarter allocation, but fairer, more transparent, and more sustainable systems.

Key Takeaway

AI in resource allocation has the potential to transform how schools and universities use their limited budgets, staff, and facilities. By forecasting needs and optimizing distribution, AI makes institutions more efficient and responsive.

Yet efficiency without equity risks deepening inequalities. Ethical implementation requires transparency, inclusivity, and human oversight. When done well, AI turns resource allocation from a political struggle into a process guided by fairness, foresight, and a commitment to serving all learners.

Enhancing Communication

Education is not only about teaching content—it is about relationships. The success of a school or university depends on effective communication among students, teachers, parents, administrators, and the wider community. Yet, communication has long been a challenge in education. Parents miss important updates, students struggle to find answers, and administrators spend hours responding to routine inquiries.

Artificial Intelligence is reshaping this landscape. From chatbots that provide instant answers to multilingual translation systems that bridge language gaps, AI tools are making communication faster, more personalized, and more inclusive. These systems reduce administrative burdens, ensure no message gets lost, and strengthen trust between schools and the communities they serve.

The Communication Gap in Education

Even before AI, schools faced significant communication challenges:

- **Information Overload:** Parents and students are bombarded with emails, notices, and online updates—often missing critical information.
- **Accessibility Barriers:** Non-native speakers or families with limited digital literacy may struggle to understand communications.
- **Response Delays:** Administrators cannot always respond quickly to thousands of inquiries.
- **Inconsistent Messaging:** Different departments may provide conflicting or incomplete information.

When communication fails, the results can be serious: missed deadlines, confusion about policies, disengaged parents, and frustrated students. AI offers tools to address these challenges by making communication systems smarter and more adaptive.

How AI Enhances Communication

AI improves communication in education through several key applications:

1. **Chatbots and Virtual Assistants**
   AI-powered chatbots provide instant answers to common questions about schedules, assignments, financial aid, or policies. Available 24/7, they reduce the burden on staff and ensure students and parents receive timely information.
2. **Multilingual Translation**
   AI translation tools break down language barriers. Parents who do not speak the school's primary language can still receive messages in their own language. Similarly, students

from immigrant families can better understand instructions and updates.

3. **Personalized Messaging**
   AI analyzes data to personalize communication. For example, parents may receive updates specific to their child's attendance, grades, or activities rather than generic newsletters. This makes messages more relevant and engaging.
4. **Predictive Communication**
   By analyzing patterns, AI can anticipate questions before they arise. For instance, if many students typically ask about exam schedules in March, the system can send proactive reminders in February.
5. **Sentiment Analysis**
   AI can analyze feedback from surveys, emails, or social media to gauge community sentiment. Schools can detect concerns early and respond strategically to maintain trust.

Case Study 1: Georgia State University's Pounce

Georgia State's AI chatbot **Pounce** is one of the most cited success stories. Originally deployed for admissions support, Pounce also helps students with financial aid, registration, and academic questions. Available by text message, it communicates in a familiar, accessible way for students.

Within its first year, Pounce responded to over **200,000 student questions**, significantly reducing summer melt and improving retention.

Case Study 2: Multilingual Parent Communication in U.S. Schools

Several school districts in the U.S. now use AI-driven translation tools to send communications in dozens of languages. Parents receive text messages, voice calls, or emails in their preferred language. This has improved parent engagement dramatically, especially in communities with large immigrant populations.

Case Study 3: AI Hotlines in UK Universities

Universities in the UK have deployed AI-powered virtual assistants on their websites and phone lines. Students can ask about course registration, housing, or mental health services at any time. One institution reported a **60% drop in routine email volume** after implementing an AI hotline.

Benefits for Students

Students benefit directly from AI-enhanced communication:

- **Instant Answers:** No waiting for office hours or email replies.
- **Reduced Anxiety:** Questions about deadlines or policies are resolved quickly.
- **Personalized Support:** Updates and reminders are tailored to their needs.
- **Accessibility:** Non-native speakers and students with disabilities can access communication in formats that work for them.

For example, a student struggling with course registration can ask a chatbot at midnight and get immediate guidance instead of missing a deadline.

Benefits for Parents

Parents also gain:

- **Stronger Engagement:** AI ensures parents are informed and involved.
- **Language Access:** Families receive communication in their preferred language.
- **Proactive Updates:** Instead of chasing information, parents receive timely reminders about attendance, grades, or events.

- **24/7 Access:** Working parents can get answers outside school hours.

This improves trust and collaboration between families and schools.

Benefits for Teachers and Administrators

For educators and administrators, AI communication tools mean:

- **Reduced Workload:** Chatbots handle routine questions, freeing staff for complex cases.
- **Consistency:** Automated systems ensure consistent, accurate messaging.
- **Community Insights:** Sentiment analysis highlights concerns before they escalate.
- **Focus on Relationships:** With routine communication automated, staff can invest more in meaningful interactions.

One administrator described AI chatbots as "our front line of communication"—filtering simple inquiries so staff can focus on human connection.

Risks and Concerns

Despite benefits, AI communication tools raise important concerns:

1. **Impersonal Interactions:** Over-reliance on chatbots may make families feel disconnected from real people.
2. **Data Privacy:** Communication systems collect sensitive information about students and families.
3. **Bias in Responses:** If chatbots are poorly designed, they may misinterpret questions or provide misleading information.
4. **Digital Divide:** Families without reliable internet or smartphones may still be left out.

These risks highlight the need for human oversight and equity-focused design.

Ethical Implementation

To implement communication AI responsibly, schools should:

- **Blend Human and AI Support:** Ensure chatbots escalate complex or sensitive issues to staff.
- **Protect Privacy:** Encrypt data and limit collection to essential information.
- **Ensure Accessibility:** Provide multiple channels (phone, text, paper) so all families are included.
- **Audit Accuracy:** Regularly test chatbot responses and translation quality.

The guiding principle is that AI should enhance—not replace—human relationships.

The Global Perspective

- **United States:** AI chatbots and translation tools are common in urban districts with diverse populations.
- **Europe:** Strong privacy laws shape cautious adoption, with emphasis on transparency.
- **Asia:** High adoption rates, especially in China, where universities use AI to manage student services at scale.
- **Developing Countries:** AI-powered SMS systems are used to send reminders about attendance, vaccinations, or exams, making communication possible even without internet.

Global variation shows how local contexts influence the balance between innovation and accessibility.

The Future of AI Communication

Looking ahead, AI may reshape communication even more profoundly:

- **Voice-Activated Assistants:** Parents and students interacting with school systems through smart speakers.
- **Emotionally Intelligent Bots:** Systems that detect frustration or confusion and respond empathetically.
- **Holistic Platforms:** Integration of chatbots, email, SMS, and social media into unified communication systems.
- **Community Analytics:** Schools using sentiment analysis to measure trust and satisfaction across stakeholders.

The future is not just faster communication—it is smarter, more empathetic, and more inclusive interaction.

Key Takeaway

Communication is the lifeblood of education, and AI makes it more efficient, accessible, and personalized. From chatbots answering student questions to translation tools connecting families, AI strengthens the bonds between schools and communities.

But communication must remain human-centered. AI is a bridge, not a replacement, ensuring that messages flow smoothly while preserving the relationships that define education. Done thoughtfully, AI communication systems foster trust, reduce barriers, and create schools where every voice can be heard.

Measuring Institutional Performance

Every education system faces the same challenge: how to know whether it is working. Schools and universities spend millions of dollars on programs, staff, and technology, but without reliable performance measurement, it is difficult to determine what actually improves student learning and institutional outcomes. Traditionally, performance has been measured through test scores, graduation rates, and rankings. These metrics, while important, capture only part of the picture.

Artificial Intelligence offers a more comprehensive, nuanced, and timely way to measure institutional performance. By analyzing vast amounts of data from students, teachers, facilities, and operations, AI systems provide real-time insights that help schools understand strengths, identify weaknesses, and guide strategic decisions. The result is not just accountability, but continuous improvement.

The Limitations of Traditional Measurement

Conventional performance measures include:

- **Standardized Test Scores:** A snapshot of academic achievement, often criticized for narrow focus.
- **Graduation and Retention Rates:** Useful but lagging indicators, showing outcomes long after interventions.
- **Rankings:** Influential in higher education but often based on limited or biased criteria.
- **Financial Reports:** Measure efficiency but not necessarily effectiveness.

These methods are retrospective, slow, and incomplete. They struggle to capture the complexity of modern education, including socio-emotional learning, equity, and long-term student outcomes.

How AI Transforms Performance Measurement

AI introduces several innovations to institutional performance tracking:

1. **Real-Time Data Analysis**
   Instead of waiting months or years for test scores or reports, AI systems analyze data continuously. Schools can track student progress, teacher performance, and resource usage in real time.
2. **Holistic Metrics**
   AI can measure a broader set of outcomes, including engagement, collaboration, creativity, and well-being. These are harder to quantify but increasingly recognized as essential.
3. **Predictive Insights**
   By identifying trends early, AI can forecast institutional performance. For example, it can predict graduation rates based on current student behavior, allowing proactive interventions.
4. **Equity Monitoring**
   AI can detect disparities in performance between different groups of students, helping schools address inequities before they widen.
5. **Operational Efficiency**
   AI tracks institutional processes—such as resource use, scheduling, and facilities management—linking operational performance with educational outcomes.

Case Study 1: Georgia State University

Georgia State is again a model of innovation. By using predictive analytics, the university not only improved student retention but also transformed how it measures success. Instead of relying solely on graduation rates, GSU tracks hundreds of indicators in real time, including advising sessions, financial aid use, and course completion patterns. This holistic approach has become central to the university's strategy.

Case Study 2: Finland's National AI Systems

Finland, known for educational excellence, has piloted AI systems that measure school performance based not just on test scores but also on well-being, teacher satisfaction, and creativity indicators. These broader metrics reflect Finland's philosophy that education is about more than academic performance.

Case Study 3: MOOCs and Online Universities

Massive Open Online Courses (MOOCs) and online universities like Coursera and Western Governors University use AI extensively to measure performance. AI tracks learner engagement, completion rates, and career outcomes for graduates. These insights inform course design and institutional priorities.

Benefits for Students

Students benefit indirectly from improved institutional performance measurement:

- **More Effective Programs:** Schools identify which initiatives genuinely help students.
- **Equity Gains:** AI highlights gaps in support for disadvantaged groups.
- **Better Learning Environments:** Institutions allocate resources more strategically, improving student experiences.
- **Faster Improvements:** Real-time insights allow for quicker adjustments to programs and teaching.

For example, if AI reveals that students in a specific course consistently disengage midway through the semester, institutions can intervene immediately rather than waiting for poor end-of-year results.

Benefits for Teachers

Teachers also benefit:

- **Clearer Feedback:** Performance is measured with richer data, not just test scores.
- **Professional Development:** AI identifies areas where teachers can grow, enabling personalized training.
- **Reduced Pressure:** Broader measures reduce reliance on high-stakes standardized tests.
- **Recognition of Impact:** Teachers' contributions beyond academics—such as mentoring or fostering engagement—can be captured.

This creates a more balanced and fair system of accountability.

Benefits for Institutions

At the institutional level, AI-driven performance measurement provides:

- **Strategic Insights:** Administrators see where investments yield the greatest impact.
- **Continuous Improvement:** Real-time data supports agile responses to challenges.
- **Transparency:** Schools can demonstrate effectiveness to governments, donors, and communities.
- **Reputation:** Better performance tracking enhances credibility and competitiveness.

Institutions that embrace AI analytics often position themselves as leaders in innovation and accountability.

Risks and Concerns

Despite potential, AI measurement systems raise concerns:

1. **Over-Surveillance:** Collecting too much data risks creating a culture of monitoring rather than learning.
2. **Narrow Metrics:** If AI systems prioritize measurable outcomes, intangible aspects of education (like creativity or empathy) may be undervalued.
3. **Data Bias:** If AI relies on biased data, performance measurement may unfairly penalize certain schools or communities.
4. **Pressure on Teachers and Students:** Excessive tracking may increase stress and reduce autonomy.

The challenge is ensuring performance measurement empowers rather than burdens.

Ethical Approaches

Ethical performance measurement requires:

- **Transparency:** Institutions must explain what is measured, why, and how results are used.
- **Inclusivity:** Performance metrics should reflect diverse values, not just efficiency.
- **Data Protection:** Student and teacher information must be safeguarded.
- **Balanced Accountability:** Use AI insights to support, not punish.

A guiding principle: measurement should foster growth, not fear.

Global Perspectives

- **United States:** Universities use AI to track retention and career outcomes but face criticism over surveillance.
- **Europe:** Stronger emphasis on well-being and holistic measures, guided by EU privacy laws.
- **Asia:** China and Singapore use AI heavily in national performance tracking, raising debates about state control.
- **Developing Nations:** AI is used to track basic access indicators, like attendance and literacy rates, where infrastructure is limited.

These diverse contexts highlight the importance of aligning AI with cultural and ethical priorities.

The Future of Institutional Performance

Looking ahead, AI measurement may evolve into:

- **Whole-Child Metrics:** Assessing social, emotional, and creative growth alongside academics.
- **Integrated Ecosystems:** Linking school data with workforce outcomes to measure long-term success.
- **Participatory Analytics:** Involving students and teachers in defining what success means.
- **Sustainability Indicators:** Measuring environmental and social responsibility in education.

The future of performance measurement is not just about numbers but about capturing the full story of education.

Key Takeaway

AI-powered performance measurement provides institutions with powerful tools to track progress, identify gaps, and drive improvement. It offers real-time insights, broader metrics, and predictive forecasting that benefit students, teachers, and administrators.

But measurement must remain human-centered. If AI reduces education to data points, it risks losing sight of learning's true purpose. Done thoughtfully, AI makes performance measurement not just about accountability, but about building schools and universities that continuously grow, adapt, and serve all learners more effectively.

CHAPTER 6

Challenges, Risks, and Responsible Use

Bias and Fairness in AI Tools

Artificial Intelligence is often described as "objective," capable of analyzing data without human subjectivity. But in reality, AI systems reflect the data and design choices of the humans who build them. If the data is biased—or if the algorithms are designed without fairness in mind—the AI will replicate and even amplify those biases.

In education, this poses serious risks. Biased AI systems can influence which students are flagged as "at risk," how work is graded, who receives extra support, or even which applicants are admitted to universities. These decisions have life-changing consequences. Ensuring fairness is therefore not just a technical challenge but a moral imperative.

Understanding Bias in AI

Bias in AI arises from several sources:

1. **Historical Data Bias**
   AI learns from past data. If historical records reflect inequalities, the system perpetuates them. For example, if certain groups have historically lower graduation rates due to systemic barriers, a predictive AI may unfairly flag those students as "likely to fail."
2. **Sampling Bias**
   If training data does not represent all student groups equally, the AI performs worse for underrepresented groups. For instance, an essay-grading system trained mostly on native English speakers may misinterpret grammar and writing style from second-language learners.
3. **Algorithmic Bias**
   Design choices by developers—such as how success is defined—introduce bias. If a system prioritizes test scores as the sole indicator of success, it undervalues creativity or collaboration.

4. **Feedback Loops**
   AI predictions can influence outcomes in self-reinforcing cycles. If an AI flags a student as "at risk," teachers may lower expectations, leading to poorer performance that confirms the AI's original prediction.

Why Fairness Matters in Education

Education is a space where fairness must be paramount. Students rely on schools to provide equal opportunities regardless of race, gender, income, or background. If AI tools reinforce inequities, they undermine the very mission of education.

Fair AI ensures:

- **Equity of Opportunity:** All students receive the support they need to succeed.
- **Trust in Institutions:** Students and families are more likely to accept AI if they believe it treats them fairly.
- **Accuracy:** Biased systems are not only unfair but also less effective, as they fail to reflect reality for diverse learners.

Case Study 1: Automated Essay Scoring

Automated essay scoring tools have been criticized for bias against students who use non-standard dialects or creative styles. Research has shown that such systems sometimes penalize African American Vernacular English (AAVE) or essays with unconventional structure, even when the content is strong.

This raises questions: Should AI prioritize conformity to standardized grammar, or should it recognize diverse expressions of thought?

Case Study 2: Proctoring Software Bias

During the pandemic, remote proctoring tools often relied on facial recognition to verify students. Students with darker skin tones reported higher rates of errors, with systems sometimes failing to detect their faces. This created unfair stress during exams and highlighted how biased training datasets can exclude entire groups.

Case Study 3: Predictive Analytics at Universities

Predictive analytics tools flag students at risk of dropping out. At some universities, minority and low-income students were disproportionately flagged, not because of their ability, but because historical data reflected structural barriers. Without careful oversight, such tools risk reinforcing stereotypes rather than addressing inequities.

The Psychological Impact of Bias

Bias in AI tools is not just technical—it affects students emotionally. Being unfairly penalized by a grading system or flagged as "at risk" can:

- Reduce confidence.
- Increase disengagement.
- Create distrust in teachers and institutions.
- Reinforce feelings of marginalization.

For vulnerable students, these effects can compound existing challenges, widening educational inequities.

Strategies to Ensure Fairness

Addressing bias in AI requires intentional effort at every stage:

1. **Diverse Data Sets**
   Training data must represent all student groups fairly. This

includes linguistic diversity, cultural variation, and a range of learning styles.

2. **Bias Audits**
   Regular, independent audits of AI systems can detect whether outputs are disproportionately disadvantaging certain groups.
3. **Human Oversight**
   AI recommendations should always be reviewed by teachers or administrators who can contextualize and override flawed decisions.
4. **Transparency**
   Students and parents must understand how AI systems work, what data is used, and what decisions are influenced.
5. **Inclusive Design Teams**
   Diverse teams of developers are more likely to anticipate and correct for bias.
6. **Focus on Equity, Not Just Efficiency**
   AI should be designed to support disadvantaged groups, even if it is less "efficient" in a narrow sense.

Benefits of Fair AI

When fairness is prioritized, AI tools can:

- Identify inequities more accurately.
- Provide targeted support for marginalized groups.
- Increase trust in technology.
- Ensure education systems fulfill their mission of equity and inclusion.

Risks of Ignoring Fairness

If fairness is ignored, AI tools can:

- Deepen educational inequities.
- Damage institutional credibility.
- Harm student well-being.
- Create legal and regulatory challenges.

The stakes are high: unfair AI in education is not just a technical flaw but a violation of students' rights.

Global Perspectives

- **United States:** Strong debates around fairness, especially in admissions, grading, and proctoring systems.
- **Europe:** Stricter regulations under GDPR demand transparency and fairness audits.
- **China:** Widespread AI adoption with less emphasis on fairness, raising concerns about systemic inequities.
- **Developing Nations:** AI tools are often imported, raising questions about whether they are adapted to local contexts.

Fairness must be defined not only technically but culturally, ensuring systems reflect diverse values and needs.

The Future of Fair AI in Education

Looking forward, fairness will remain central to AI adoption in schools. Innovations may include:

- **Explainable AI:** Systems that can explain their decisions in human terms, making bias easier to detect.
- **Adaptive Fairness Models:** AI that adjusts outputs to ensure equity across groups.
- **Student-Centered AI:** Systems designed with student voices involved in development.
- **Global Standards:** International frameworks ensuring fairness across borders.

Fairness is not an add-on but a foundation. Without it, AI risks betraying education's promise of equal opportunity.

Key Takeaway

AI tools in education hold enormous potential—but they are not neutral. Bias creeps in through data, design, and deployment, and if unchecked, it can reinforce inequities rather than reduce them. Ensuring fairness requires diverse data, ethical design, human oversight, and a commitment to equity above efficiency.

The future of AI in education depends on fairness. If systems are fair, they can unlock new opportunities for all learners. If they are not, they risk becoming another barrier in the long struggle for educational justice.

Ethical AI Adoption Policies

Artificial Intelligence is no longer a futuristic idea—it is already embedded in classrooms, admissions offices, and administrative systems worldwide. Yet while the technology advances rapidly, policies governing its ethical use often lag behind. Schools and universities face a critical question: how do we adopt AI tools in ways that maximize benefits while minimizing harm?

Without clear policies, institutions risk biased decision-making, privacy violations, or loss of trust among students and families. Ethical adoption is not just about compliance with laws—it is about aligning AI use with the values of education: equity, fairness, trust, and human growth.

Why Policies Matter

The adoption of AI in education raises complex questions:

- Who owns the data collected by AI systems?
- How are students informed about AI's role in their education?
- What safeguards exist against bias or errors?
- How do institutions balance innovation with accountability?

Policies provide the framework to answer these questions. They set boundaries, define responsibilities, and ensure that technology serves human needs rather than the other way around.

The Principles of Ethical AI Adoption

Several core principles guide responsible AI use in education:

1. **Transparency**
   Schools must be open about how AI is used, what data is collected, and how decisions are made. Students and parents should not be left in the dark.
2. **Accountability**
   Institutions must take responsibility for AI decisions. Blaming "the algorithm" is not acceptable—humans remain accountable.
3. **Fairness**
   AI systems must be audited for bias and designed to promote equity. Policies must ensure they do not reinforce systemic inequalities.
4. **Privacy**
   Data collection should be minimized, secured, and consent-based. Students must retain rights over their information.
5. **Human Oversight**
   AI should support, not replace, human judgment. Teachers, counselors, and administrators must remain the final decision-makers.
6. **Inclusivity**
   Policies should ensure that AI serves all students, including those with disabilities, language barriers, or limited access to technology.
7. **Continuous Evaluation**
   AI systems should be regularly reviewed to ensure they remain effective, fair, and aligned with institutional values.

Case Study 1: UNESCO's AI in Education Guidelines

In 2021, UNESCO released global guidelines emphasizing equity, inclusion, and transparency in educational AI. The guidelines stress that AI should never undermine human rights and that schools must adopt policies to safeguard privacy and prevent bias. Many countries now use these as a baseline for national strategies.

Case Study 2: The European Union's AI Act

The EU's proposed AI Act categorizes education-related AI systems as "high risk," requiring strict oversight. Institutions must conduct risk assessments, ensure transparency, and provide human review mechanisms. This framework reflects a proactive policy approach where ethics is built into regulation.

Case Study 3: U.S. University Policies

Some U.S. universities have begun drafting AI ethics policies independently. For example, Stanford and MIT have issued guidelines emphasizing transparency and fairness in admissions algorithms, grading tools, and student support systems. These policies include commitments to bias audits and student consent.

Why Institutions Struggle

Despite progress, many institutions face challenges in developing policies:

- **Rapid Change:** AI evolves faster than policy cycles.
- **Limited Expertise:** Schools often lack staff trained in AI ethics.
- **Vendor Dependence:** Institutions rely on private companies whose business models may prioritize profit over fairness.
- **Global Variation:** Different legal frameworks complicate cross-border consistency.

These challenges mean many schools adopt AI reactively, without comprehensive ethical frameworks in place.

Building an Ethical AI Policy Framework

An effective policy framework typically includes:

1. **Governance Structures**
   Establishing ethics committees or AI oversight boards composed of educators, technologists, parents, and students.
2. **Data Governance**
   Defining who owns student data, how it is stored, and what rights students have to access or delete it.
3. **Bias Audits**
   Requiring regular independent evaluations of AI tools to detect and correct unfair outcomes.
4. **Human-in-the-Loop Systems**
   Ensuring that all high-stakes decisions (admissions, grading, interventions) are reviewed by humans.
5. **Training and Awareness**
   Providing teachers and staff with training in AI literacy and ethics so they can use systems responsibly.
6. **Student Rights**
   Guaranteeing that students are informed about AI use and have avenues to challenge or appeal AI-driven decisions.
7. **Vendor Accountability**
   Requiring contracts with technology providers to include ethical standards, data protection requirements, and transparency obligations.

Benefits of Ethical Adoption Policies

When schools adopt clear policies, they gain:

- **Trust:** Students and families feel safer engaging with AI tools.
- **Fairness:** Bias is reduced, ensuring equitable opportunities.

- **Efficiency with Safeguards:** Innovation is encouraged without sacrificing rights.
- **Legal Protection:** Institutions reduce risks of lawsuits or regulatory violations.
- **Reputation:** Schools with strong ethics policies are seen as leaders in responsible innovation.

Risks of Policy Gaps

Without clear policies, institutions risk:

- **Unfair Outcomes:** Bias goes unchecked, disadvantaging marginalized groups.
- **Data Exploitation:** Student information may be misused by third-party vendors.
- **Loss of Trust:** Families may resist or reject AI adoption.
- **Legal Trouble:** Non-compliance with regulations like GDPR or FERPA.
- **Missed Opportunities:** Schools may hesitate to adopt AI at all due to fear of ethical pitfalls.

The Role of Teachers and Students

Policies are most effective when teachers and students are involved in their creation. Teachers must be trained not just in how to use AI tools, but in how to question their fairness and accuracy. Students should have a voice in defining what ethical AI looks like, since they are the ones most affected.

Global Perspectives

- **Europe:** Strong regulatory frameworks lead the way, with policies emphasizing fairness and privacy.
- **United States:** More fragmented, with policies varying across states and institutions.
- **China:** Heavy use of AI in education but weaker emphasis on ethics, raising concerns about surveillance.

- **Developing Nations:** Often adopt AI tools before policies are in place, leading to risks of exploitation or inequity.

The global picture shows that ethical adoption requires both local leadership and international collaboration.

The Future of AI Policies in Education

Looking forward, policies may evolve toward:

- **International Standards:** Agreements ensuring fairness across borders.
- **Student Data Ownership Models:** Systems where students fully control their educational data.
- **Continuous Auditing:** AI tools that include built-in fairness checks.
- **Participatory Governance:** Schools involving students, parents, and communities in oversight.

The future of AI in education depends not only on technology but on the rules and values guiding its use.

Key Takeaway

AI adoption without ethical policies risks undermining fairness, privacy, and trust in education. Clear frameworks—emphasizing transparency, accountability, equity, and human oversight—are essential.

Policies should not be seen as barriers to innovation but as enablers of sustainable, fair, and trusted AI adoption. With the right safeguards, AI can enhance education without compromising its core mission: empowering every learner.

Teacher and Student Resistance

Artificial Intelligence promises to transform education—but not everyone is ready to embrace it. While policymakers and technologists often highlight efficiency, personalization, and innovation, teachers and students sometimes respond with skepticism, fear, or outright resistance. These reactions are not trivial barriers; they reflect real concerns about autonomy, identity, and trust in education.

Understanding resistance is essential. If schools push AI adoption without addressing fears, they risk alienating the very people these systems are meant to serve. But when institutions engage with resistance openly, they can build confidence, create better systems, and ensure adoption is both effective and ethical.

Why Teachers Resist AI

Teachers sit at the heart of education, and their concerns about AI often stem from deep professional values. Key sources of resistance include:

1. **Fear of Replacement**
   Perhaps the most common concern is that AI will replace teachers. Headlines about "robot tutors" or "automated classrooms" fuel anxiety that schools may devalue human educators. Teachers worry about job security and about being reduced to supervisors of machines.
2. **Loss of Autonomy**
   Teachers are professionals who value judgment, creativity, and personal connection. If AI dictates pacing, content, or grading, some fear they will lose control over their classrooms.
3. **Skepticism About Accuracy**
   Teachers often doubt whether AI can truly understand complex student needs. Concerns include grading errors, misidentifying at-risk students, or misinterpreting emotions.

4. **Workload Concerns**
   Ironically, while AI promises to reduce workload, many teachers fear it will add to it. Learning new systems, troubleshooting glitches, and managing data dashboards can initially increase stress.
5. **Ethical Worries**
   Teachers often feel protective of their students. They may resist AI because they worry about privacy, fairness, and the commercialization of education.

Why Students Resist AI

Students, too, express reservations about AI in education. Their concerns often differ from teachers', but they are equally important:

1. **Surveillance Anxiety**
   AI tools that track clicks, facial expressions, or test behavior can feel invasive. Students may fear constant monitoring, reducing their sense of safety and freedom.
2. **Trust in Fairness**
   Students may not believe AI systems grade fairly, especially if they write creatively, use non-standard language, or express themselves in unique ways.
3. **Fear of Dehumanization**
   Students often value human connection in education. They worry AI tutors or automated feedback will make learning feel cold and mechanical.
4. **Digital Divide**
   Students from low-income families may resist AI if they lack access to devices or internet at home. They may perceive AI as another tool that advantages wealthier peers.
5. **Job Market Concerns**
   Some students fear that if AI is teaching them, they may be unprepared for real-world, human-centered work. They want reassurance that their education remains relevant.

Case Study 1: Remote Proctoring Backlash

During the pandemic, universities adopted AI proctoring tools to monitor online exams. Students protested, citing surveillance, anxiety, and bias against certain demographics. Some universities faced petitions with thousands of signatures demanding removal of these tools.

This backlash illustrates how resistance grows when AI adoption feels imposed rather than collaborative.

Case Study 2: Teacher Unions and Automation

In several countries, teacher unions have raised alarms about AI tools replacing core aspects of teaching. In the UK, unions pushed back against algorithmic grading during COVID-19, when an automated system downgraded many students unfairly. Teacher resistance in this case was critical in forcing governments to revise policies.

The Psychology of Resistance

Resistance is not just practical—it is psychological. Several theories help explain why teachers and students resist AI:

- **Loss Aversion:** People fear losing autonomy, identity, or privacy more than they value potential gains.
- **Change Fatigue:** Education has experienced decades of reforms. Teachers and students may see AI as "just another initiative" that will fade, leading to skepticism.
- **Trust Deficit:** If institutions adopt AI without transparency, resistance increases because people do not trust hidden systems.
- **Threat to Identity:** Teachers see themselves as mentors, not data managers. Students see themselves as learners, not data points. AI can feel like a threat to these identities.

Strategies to Address Teacher Resistance

1. **Position AI as Support, Not Replacement**
   Schools must emphasize that AI will assist teachers, not replace them. Framing AI as a "co-teacher" or "assistant" helps reduce fear.
2. **Provide Training and Agency**
   Teachers should receive training not just in how to use AI but in how to control it. When teachers feel ownership, resistance decreases.
3. **Involve Teachers in Design**
   Educators should be consulted when choosing or designing AI tools. This ensures systems align with classroom realities.
4. **Showcase Success Stories**
   Peer-to-peer examples are powerful. Teachers are more likely to embrace AI if they see colleagues using it successfully.
5. **Respect Ethical Concerns**
   Policies must address privacy, bias, and equity openly. Teachers need assurance their students are protected.

Strategies to Address Student Resistance

1. **Transparency About Data**
   Students should know what data is collected, why, and how it benefits them. Clear explanations build trust.
2. **Choice and Agency**
   Where possible, students should have the option to opt out of certain tools or choose how they engage with AI systems.
3. **Human Connection First**
   AI should never replace human feedback entirely. Maintaining strong teacher-student relationships reduces fears of dehumanization.
4. **Address Equity Issues**
   Schools must provide access to devices and internet to ensure no student is disadvantaged.
5. **Highlight Benefits**
   Students should see tangible benefits—like faster feedback,

personalized learning, or reduced anxiety about grades—to recognize AI as helpful.

Benefits of Overcoming Resistance

When resistance is addressed, adoption is smoother and outcomes are stronger. Teachers who initially feared AI often become advocates when they see workload reductions. Students who distrust AI can embrace it once they experience fairness and personalization.

Overcoming resistance builds a culture of trust, where AI is not seen as a threat but as a partner in education.

Risks of Ignoring Resistance

If schools push AI without addressing concerns, risks include:

- **Low Adoption:** Teachers may ignore or underuse tools.
- **Distrust:** Students and parents may lose faith in institutions.
- **Backlash:** Protests, petitions, or union resistance can derail adoption.
- **Inequity:** Students without resources may be further disadvantaged.

Ignoring resistance often leads to failed implementation—even when the technology itself is promising.

Global Perspectives

- **United States:** Teacher unions and student activists often lead resistance, especially around privacy and equity.
- **Europe:** Strong privacy laws reflect cultural skepticism toward surveillance-heavy AI.
- **Asia:** Faster adoption in countries like China and South Korea, but with growing student pushback against exam-monitoring tools.

- **Developing Nations:** Resistance often stems from infrastructure gaps, with students wary of tools that highlight inequality.

Resistance looks different globally but reflects the same core concern: protecting human dignity in education.

The Future of Resistance and Trust

As AI becomes more common, resistance will not disappear—but it can evolve into **critical engagement**. Instead of rejecting AI outright, teachers and students may demand systems that meet higher ethical standards. This could drive innovation toward more human-centered, transparent, and equitable tools.

The future may see schools adopting **participatory AI governance**, where students, teachers, and parents help decide which tools to use and how. This approach transforms resistance from an obstacle into a catalyst for better design.

Key Takeaway

Resistance to AI in education is not irrational—it is a rational response to fears about autonomy, fairness, and identity. Teachers worry about losing their professional role; students fear surveillance and dehumanization.

The path forward is not to dismiss resistance but to engage with it. Schools must emphasize transparency, human oversight, and shared decision-making. When resistance is respected, it becomes a source of valuable feedback, ensuring AI serves education's true mission: empowering people, not replacing them.

Legal and Regulatory Challenges

Artificial Intelligence is transforming education, but with transformation comes regulation. Schools and universities do not operate in a vacuum—they must comply with laws protecting student rights, privacy, equity, and intellectual property. Yet the legal landscape for AI in education is complex and constantly evolving. Regulations differ across countries, technology often outpaces legislation, and institutions struggle to interpret how existing laws apply to new AI tools.

The challenge for schools is twofold: adopt AI in ways that maximize innovation, while ensuring compliance with legal and regulatory frameworks. Failure to do so risks lawsuits, reputational damage, and most importantly, harm to students.

The Core Legal Issues

Several legal areas intersect with AI in education:

1. **Data Privacy and Protection**
   AI systems rely on vast amounts of student data—academic records, demographic information, behavior logs, sometimes even biometric data. Laws like **FERPA** (U.S.) and **GDPR** (EU) place strict limits on how this data can be collected, stored, and shared. Non-compliance carries heavy penalties.
2. **Equity and Non-Discrimination**
   Education is legally required to provide equal opportunities. If AI systems discriminate—intentionally or not—they can violate anti-discrimination laws. For example, if predictive analytics flag minority students as "at risk" disproportionately, institutions may face legal challenges.
3. **Intellectual Property (IP)**
   AI-generated content raises questions of ownership. If an AI tool generates lesson plans or assessments, who owns the material—the teacher, the school, or the software company?

In higher education, this extends to research and academic publishing.

4. **Accessibility**
   Laws like the **Americans with Disabilities Act (ADA)** in the U.S. require schools to provide accessible education. AI tools that fail to accommodate students with disabilities may face legal scrutiny.
5. **Surveillance and Consent**
   AI systems that monitor student behavior—such as proctoring tools or facial recognition—raise questions about consent and surveillance. In some regions, these tools may be legally restricted or banned.

Case Study 1: The 2020 UK Grading Scandal

During the COVID-19 pandemic, the UK government used an algorithm to assign exam grades when tests were canceled. The system disproportionately downgraded students from disadvantaged schools, sparking national outrage. Legal challenges argued that the algorithm violated principles of fairness and equal opportunity. The government eventually reversed the decision.

This case shows how regulatory frameworks must guard against unfair automated decision-making.

Case Study 2: U.S. FERPA Violations

Several EdTech companies in the U.S. have faced lawsuits for violating the **Family Educational Rights and Privacy Act (FERPA)** by sharing student data with third parties without consent. These cases highlight the legal risks of commercial exploitation of student data.

Case Study 3: EU GDPR and Education AI

Under the **General Data Protection Regulation (GDPR)**, European schools face strict rules on data minimization, consent, and transparency. An AI system that collects excessive student data or fails to explain its decision-making may be deemed unlawful. This has made European institutions more cautious in AI adoption.

The Global Legal Landscape

- **United States**: A patchwork of laws (FERPA, COPPA, ADA) regulate data and equity, but there is no comprehensive national AI law. Much responsibility falls on states and institutions.
- **European Union**: The AI Act (pending) categorizes education AI as "high risk," requiring bias audits, transparency, and human oversight. GDPR already provides strong protections.
- **China**: Rapid AI adoption in education is encouraged by the government, but privacy protections are weaker. Critics warn of surveillance-heavy practices.
- **Developing Nations**: Many countries lack strong AI-specific laws, raising risks of unregulated adoption and exploitation by private companies.

The global picture shows stark differences: while Europe prioritizes regulation, the U.S. and China push faster adoption, with uneven safeguards.

Key Challenges Institutions Face

1. **Unclear Laws**
   Many existing laws predate AI and do not explicitly address its use in education. Schools often operate in gray areas.
2. **Vendor Compliance**
   Schools rely heavily on private AI vendors, but contracts may lack clarity on data ownership, security, or liability. Institutions bear legal risk when vendors fail.
3. **Cross-Border Data**
   Cloud-based AI systems often store data globally, raising conflicts between jurisdictions with different privacy standards.

4. **Rapid Change**
   Technology evolves faster than regulation, leaving gaps where harmful practices can emerge before laws catch up.
5. **Accountability**
   When AI makes mistakes, who is legally responsible? The teacher? The institution? The vendor? Policies often lack clarity.

Strategies for Compliance

To navigate the legal landscape, schools and universities must adopt proactive strategies:

1. **Legal Literacy**
   Educators and administrators must be trained to understand relevant laws and how they apply to AI.
2. **Robust Contracts**
   Agreements with vendors should include clear terms on data ownership, privacy, and accountability.
3. **Data Protection Officers**
   Many institutions now appoint data protection officers (DPOs) to oversee compliance and act as watchdogs.
4. **Bias and Fairness Audits**
   Regular audits ensure AI systems comply with anti-discrimination laws.
5. **Student Consent and Rights**
   Policies should guarantee students are informed and can challenge AI-driven decisions.
6. **Alignment with Global Standards**
   Even in countries with weak laws, schools can adopt best practices from stricter frameworks like GDPR.

Benefits of Strong Legal Compliance

- **Trust:** Students and families are more willing to accept AI when rights are protected.
- **Equity:** Compliance with anti-discrimination laws ensures fairer outcomes.

- **Security:** Strong data protections prevent breaches and misuse.
- **Reputation:** Institutions seen as ethical leaders gain credibility.
- **Sustainability:** Compliance reduces risks of sudden bans or lawsuits.

Risks of Ignoring Regulation

Ignoring legal frameworks can result in:

- **Lawsuits and Penalties:** Institutions face heavy fines under GDPR or FERPA violations.
- **Loss of Trust:** Families may resist AI adoption if rights are violated.
- **Policy Backlash:** Governments may impose stricter restrictions if abuses occur.
- **Harm to Students:** Privacy violations or unfair outcomes can have long-term consequences for learners.

The Future of AI Regulation in Education

Looking ahead, regulation will likely expand in several directions:

- **Comprehensive AI Laws:** Many countries are drafting new legislation specific to AI.
- **Global Standards:** International organizations may push for harmonized protections.
- **Explainability Requirements:** Laws may require AI systems to explain decisions in plain language.
- **Student Rights Expansion:** Students may gain new rights to data ownership, algorithmic transparency, and appeals.
- **Public Accountability:** Schools may be required to publish audits of AI tools used.

The balance will be delicate: too little regulation risks harm; too much may stifle innovation.

Key Takeaway

Legal and regulatory challenges are not side issues—they are central to AI in education. Institutions must navigate privacy laws, equity requirements, accessibility mandates, and intellectual property rules, all while keeping pace with rapid technological change.

The path forward lies in proactive compliance, ethical contracting, and alignment with global best practices. Innovation without regulation risks harming students; regulation without innovation risks stagnation. The goal is balance: ensuring AI advances education while protecting the rights and dignity of every learner.

CHAPTER 7

The Future of AI in Education

Emerging Technologies on the Horizon

Artificial Intelligence in education today already feels transformative, but we are still only at the beginning. The next decade will bring technologies that push far beyond adaptive learning platforms or automated grading. From AI tutors indistinguishable from humans to immersive virtual classrooms and even brain-computer interfaces, the horizon of possibilities is expanding rapidly.

For schools and universities, this is both exciting and daunting. These emerging tools could redefine how students learn, how teachers teach, and even what it means to be educated. Yet they also raise profound ethical, social, and philosophical questions. Understanding these technologies now helps educators prepare not just for adoption, but for guiding them toward responsible use.

AI Tutors and Companions

Perhaps the most anticipated development is the rise of **AI tutors**—systems capable of interacting with students conversationally, answering questions, explaining concepts, and offering feedback much like a human tutor.

Unlike today's limited chatbots, future AI tutors will combine natural language processing, emotional intelligence, and adaptive algorithms to create personalized learning companions.

- **How They Work:** AI tutors analyze a student's progress, detect misunderstandings, and provide explanations tailored to learning style.
- **Potential Benefits:** Every student gains access to one-on-one tutoring, something only wealthy families could afford in the past.
- **Challenges:** Risks include over-reliance, reduced human interaction, and questions about whether AI tutors can truly replicate empathy.

Example: Imagine a high school student struggling with algebra. An AI tutor patiently explains concepts in multiple ways, tracks progress over weeks, and celebrates milestones—all at no extra cost to the school.

Virtual and Augmented Reality Classrooms

Virtual Reality (VR) and **Augmented Reality (AR)** are merging with AI to create immersive educational environments. Instead of reading about history, students can "walk" through ancient Rome. Instead of watching a science video, they can manipulate molecules in 3D space.

AI enhances VR/AR by personalizing experiences. For example, an AI system might adjust the difficulty of a VR physics experiment based on how quickly a student grasps concepts.

- **Potential Benefits:** Deep engagement, experiential learning, and opportunities to explore subjects impossible to replicate in real life.
- **Challenges:** Cost, accessibility, and risk of prioritizing spectacle over substance.

Case Example: Medical schools already use VR simulations for surgery training, with AI providing real-time feedback on precision and technique.

Brain-Computer Interfaces (BCIs)

One of the most futuristic developments is the rise of **brain-computer interfaces**—devices that connect the human brain directly to digital systems. While still experimental, BCIs could allow students to control devices with thought, or even accelerate learning by monitoring cognitive load in real time.

- **Potential Benefits:** BCIs could help students with disabilities communicate or interact with educational tools.

They may also provide unprecedented insights into how learning happens in the brain.
- **Challenges:** Ethical concerns around privacy, autonomy, and "hacking the brain." Schools must tread carefully to ensure such technology respects human dignity.

Speculative Example: A student practicing foreign language vocabulary might use a BCI to track which words trigger the strongest memory signals, tailoring practice sessions accordingly.

Emotionally Intelligent AI

Current AI systems are good at analyzing text and numbers, but the future will see systems capable of detecting and responding to human emotions. Using facial recognition, voice analysis, and physiological signals, emotionally intelligent AI could adjust teaching in real time.

- **Potential Benefits:** If a student appears frustrated, the system can slow down. If engagement drops, it can change strategy.
- **Challenges:** Risks of misinterpretation, invasiveness, and surveillance-like monitoring.

This raises a key question: should schools allow machines to interpret emotions, or does that cross ethical boundaries?

Generative AI for Creativity

Today's generative AI—capable of producing essays, images, or music—is just the beginning. Future systems will co-create with students, helping them brainstorm, design, and produce original work.

- **Potential Benefits:** Students can explore creative ideas more rapidly, gaining feedback and inspiration.
- **Challenges:** Risks of plagiarism, homogenization of creativity, and diminished human originality.

Case Example: A design student might use generative AI to quickly prototype 3D models, then refine them with human creativity.

Lifelong and Workplace Learning Platforms

Education is no longer confined to childhood. Emerging AI platforms will deliver **lifelong, personalized education** to adults, adapting to career changes and evolving industries.

- **AI in Workforce Training:** Platforms already track skill gaps and suggest training modules. In the future, these may anticipate future job markets and proactively reskill workers.
- **Global Reach:** Low-cost AI tutors could bring lifelong learning to billions worldwide.

This democratization of learning could close global skills gaps—but only if equitable access is ensured.

Ethical and Social Implications

Emerging technologies carry profound risks if not handled responsibly:

1. **Equity Gaps**
   If only wealthy schools access advanced tools like VR or AI tutors, inequality may worsen.
2. **Privacy Intrusions**
   Emotion-sensing AI and BCIs raise unprecedented questions about mental privacy.
3. **Teacher Redefinition**
   As AI takes on more instructional roles, what becomes of teachers? Are they guides, mentors, or facilitators in this new landscape?
4. **Dependency and Authenticity**
   If students rely heavily on AI tutors or generative tools, do they risk losing critical thinking and independence?

5. **Cultural Shifts**
   AI tutors may reflect dominant cultural values, raising questions about representation and inclusivity.

Global Perspectives

- **United States:** Heavy investment in EdTech startups experimenting with VR, generative AI, and AI tutors.
- **Europe:** Adoption tempered by strong ethical debates and regulatory caution.
- **China:** Rapid government-driven adoption, with heavy integration of AI into national education strategies.
- **Developing Nations:** Opportunities to leapfrog traditional systems, but risks of dependency on global technology providers.

Preparing for the Horizon

Educators and policymakers must prepare now for these emerging technologies by:

- **Developing Ethical Guidelines:** Proactively addressing privacy, equity, and fairness.
- **Investing in Infrastructure:** Ensuring access across diverse schools and communities.
- **Training Teachers:** Equipping educators to integrate emerging tools responsibly.
- **Involving Students:** Giving learners a voice in how new technologies are used.

The Future Vision

In 10–20 years, classrooms may look radically different. Students could enter VR labs guided by AI tutors who understand both their cognitive progress and emotional state. Teachers could act as facilitators, ensuring that learning remains human-centered. Lifelong learners may access personalized pathways updated in real time by global AI systems.

The promise is vast: education that is more personal, inclusive, and effective than ever before. But the challenge is equally great: ensuring these tools enhance, rather than replace, the human essence of learning.

Key Takeaway

Emerging technologies like AI tutors, VR classrooms, BCIs, and emotionally intelligent systems promise to revolutionize education. They expand possibilities for personalization, creativity, and access.

But these advances raise pressing ethical questions. Schools must adopt them thoughtfully, with fairness, privacy, and humanity at the center. The horizon of AI in education is not just about what is possible—but about what kind of learning future we choose to create.

Preparing Students for an AI-Driven World

Artificial Intelligence is no longer confined to laboratories or science fiction. It is embedded in daily life: from recommendation engines and voice assistants to workplace automation and advanced healthcare. For students entering the workforce in the coming decades, AI will not be an add-on—it will be the environment they live and work in.

This reality demands a radical shift in education. Schools and universities must prepare students not just to use AI tools, but to understand, question, and collaborate with them. Success in an AI-driven world will require technical literacy, critical thinking, creativity, and ethical judgment. The challenge is clear: how can education equip students for a future where AI is everywhere?

The Skills Students Will Need

Preparing students for an AI-driven future means focusing on a new mix of skills that go beyond traditional academics:

1. **AI Literacy**
   Students must understand how AI works at a conceptual level. This includes:

- What algorithms are and how they make decisions.
- How data is collected and used.
- The potential biases and limitations of AI systems.

This literacy does not mean every student must become a programmer—but all should understand AI's influence in society.

2. **Critical Thinking**
   In a world where machines provide answers, the ability to question becomes more important than ever. Students must learn to evaluate AI outputs, challenge assumptions, and distinguish between reliable and flawed results.
3. **Creativity and Problem-Solving**
   AI excels at pattern recognition but struggles with originality and complex human problems. Students must cultivate creativity, innovation, and interdisciplinary thinking.
4. **Ethical Awareness**
   Future citizens must grapple with ethical dilemmas: When should AI be trusted? How should privacy be protected? What is fair use of AI in work and education?
5. **Collaboration Skills**
   The future workplace will involve "human-AI collaboration." Students must learn to work not just with other people, but with intelligent systems as teammates.
6. **Adaptability and Lifelong Learning**
   With industries evolving rapidly, the ability to reskill throughout life is essential. Education must teach students how to learn, unlearn, and relearn.

Case Study 1: Finland's AI Literacy Program

Finland launched a national initiative to teach the basics of AI to its citizens. The online course "Elements of AI" has reached hundreds of thousands worldwide. While aimed at the general population, it sets a model for integrating AI literacy into education at all levels.

Case Study 2: Singapore's AI in Schools Strategy

Singapore has introduced AI-focused curricula in secondary schools, teaching coding, data science, and ethical AI use. This prepares students not only to understand AI but to lead in its development.

Case Study 3: U.S. K–12 AI Initiatives

Some U.S. school districts are piloting AI literacy programs, teaching students how machine learning works through simple projects. For example, students train AI models to recognize animals in images, learning both the potential and the limits of machine learning.

Teaching AI Without Fear

One challenge is ensuring AI education does not create fear. Students often hear alarming headlines about robots taking jobs. While automation will reshape the workforce, AI will also create new opportunities. Education must balance realism with optimism—emphasizing how students can thrive by developing human strengths AI cannot replace.

Ethical and Civic Education

Preparing students for an AI-driven world is not only about skills but about values. As future citizens, they must be able to participate in democratic debates about AI's role in society. This requires:

- Understanding bias and fairness in AI.
- Debating privacy, surveillance, and consent.
- Discussing the impact of AI on jobs and inequality.
- Exploring global perspectives on AI governance.

By embedding AI into civic education, schools prepare students not just to use technology, but to shape its future.

The Role of Teachers

Teachers themselves must be prepared to guide students into the AI era. This means professional development in AI literacy, access to resources, and a shift in teaching philosophy. Teachers will not need to know everything about AI, but they must feel confident facilitating discussions, projects, and ethical debates.

The Role of Higher Education

Universities will play a dual role:

1. Training future AI professionals with technical depth.
2. Equipping all students—whether in business, arts, or healthcare—with AI literacy and ethical awareness.

This requires integrating AI across disciplines, not siloing it within computer science.

Challenges in Preparing Students

1. **Digital Divide**
   Students without access to devices or internet risk being left behind. Preparing all students requires addressing infrastructure gaps.
2. **Curriculum Overload**
   Teachers already face packed curricula. Integrating AI education requires rethinking priorities, not simply adding more content.
3. **Teacher Readiness**
   Many educators feel unprepared to teach AI concepts. Professional development is critical.
4. **Rapid Change**
   By the time curricula are written, technology may have shifted. Schools need flexible approaches to stay current.

Strategies for Success

To overcome these challenges, schools can:

- **Start Early:** Introduce AI literacy in primary school through playful, project-based learning.
- **Use Interdisciplinary Approaches:** Teach AI concepts in math, science, social studies, and even art.
- **Prioritize Ethics:** Make ethical discussions central, not optional.
- **Leverage Partnerships:** Collaborate with tech companies, universities, and NGOs to provide resources.
- **Empower Students as Creators:** Encourage students to build, test, and critique AI tools, not just use them passively.

The Future of AI Preparation

Looking ahead, education systems may evolve into:

- **AI Across the Curriculum:** Every subject integrates AI-related discussions.
- **Student AI Portfolios:** Learners showcase AI projects and critical reflections as part of graduation requirements.
- **Global AI Literacy Standards:** International frameworks ensure all students, regardless of country, gain basic AI understanding.
- **Personalized AI Coaches:** Ironically, AI itself may help prepare students for an AI world, guiding them through adaptive learning pathways.

Key Takeaway

Preparing students for an AI-driven world is about more than teaching technology—it is about shaping resilient, creative, and ethical citizens. Students must learn to understand AI, work alongside it, and question it critically.

If schools succeed, future generations will not be passive consumers of AI but active shapers of a world where technology serves humanity. If they fail, the gap between those who understand AI and those who do not will deepen inequality.

The mission is clear: prepare students not just for jobs, but for life in an AI-shaped society.

Global Case Studies

Artificial Intelligence in education is not unfolding in a single way across the world. Each country brings its own cultural values, policy frameworks, and resource constraints to the adoption of AI tools. Studying these global approaches provides valuable lessons: what works, what doesn't, and what principles should guide the future.

By comparing case studies from diverse contexts—wealthy and developing nations, democratic and authoritarian systems, innovation-driven and resource-constrained schools—we gain insight into both the promise and the pitfalls of AI in education.

Case Study 1: United States — Innovation with Fragmentation

The U.S. has one of the most active AI in education landscapes, driven by EdTech startups, universities, and philanthropic investment.

- **Strengths:**
  - Strong private sector innovation (e.g., Gradescope, Coursera, Duolingo).
  - Universities leading in predictive analytics to improve retention.
  - Increasing experimentation with AI tutors and adaptive learning platforms.
- **Weaknesses:**
  - Fragmented policy environment, with no national AI education strategy.
  - Significant disparities between wealthy and underfunded schools.
  - Student and teacher resistance to surveillance-heavy tools (e.g., remote proctoring).

Lesson: Innovation flourishes in the U.S., but without national coordination, equity gaps risk widening.

Case Study 2: Finland — Human-Centered AI

Finland is often a model of progressive education, and its approach to AI reflects this philosophy.

- **Strengths:**
  - National programs like *Elements of AI* aim to make the entire population AI literate.
  - Emphasis on ethics, inclusion, and well-being, not just efficiency.
  - Integration of AI into lifelong learning beyond K–12.
- **Weaknesses:**
  - Slow pace of large-scale implementation due to caution and consultation.
  - Heavy reliance on government investment, limiting speed of private innovation.

Lesson: Finland shows that AI adoption can prioritize values like equity and human dignity, even if it means slower rollout.

Case Study 3: China — Scale and Surveillance

China has pursued one of the most ambitious AI in education strategies, integrating AI into classrooms at scale.

- **Strengths:**
  - Massive government funding for AI EdTech companies.
  - Use of AI tutors and adaptive platforms to supplement crowded classrooms.
  - National policy alignment, ensuring rapid adoption across regions.
- **Weaknesses:**
  - Heavy emphasis on monitoring (e.g., facial recognition to track student attention).
  - Privacy and ethical concerns often sidelined in favor of efficiency.

    - Risk of reinforcing test-driven culture through AI tools.

Lesson: China demonstrates the potential of AI at scale, but also the dangers of prioritizing control over student autonomy.

Case Study 4: Singapore — Strategic and Balanced

Singapore combines innovation with strong policy frameworks.

- **Strengths:**
    - National AI Strategy includes education as a core focus.
    - Strong teacher training to integrate AI tools effectively.
    - Balanced emphasis on technical skills, ethics, and creativity.
- **Weaknesses:**
    - Small size and centralized system make replication difficult in larger countries.
    - Risk of creating high-pressure environments through performance tracking.

Lesson: Singapore offers a model for strategic, government-led integration, balancing efficiency with ethics.

Case Study 5: India — Leapfrogging with Constraints

India faces unique challenges: a vast population, limited resources in rural areas, and uneven access to technology. Yet AI adoption is helping bridge gaps.

- **Strengths:**
    - AI-powered adaptive learning apps (e.g., BYJU'S) reach millions of students.
    - NGOs use AI to allocate scarce resources like textbooks or tutors.

- Government interest in scaling low-cost AI literacy programs.
- **Weaknesses:**
  - Digital divide remains a major obstacle.
  - Many AI tools are private-sector driven, raising concerns about commercialization.

Lesson: India shows how AI can help leapfrog traditional barriers, but equitable access remains the biggest challenge.

Case Study 6: Rwanda — Innovation in Developing Nations

Rwanda has emerged as a leader in educational technology in Africa, with strong government commitment.

- **Strengths:**
  - Partnerships with global organizations bring AI-powered tools to schools.
  - Focus on using AI for basic literacy and numeracy, tailored to local needs.
  - Integration of teacher training in EdTech adoption.
- **Weaknesses:**
  - Limited infrastructure in rural areas.
  - Dependence on international donors for funding.

Lesson: Even resource-constrained nations can harness AI effectively with government vision and global partnerships.

Comparing Approaches

1. **Policy Alignment vs. Fragmentation**
   - Countries like China and Singapore adopt AI faster due to centralized strategies.
   - Countries like the U.S. show innovation but face fragmentation.
2. **Equity vs. Efficiency**

- Finland and Rwanda emphasize equity and inclusion.
    - China prioritizes scale and efficiency, sometimes at the expense of rights.
3. **Private vs. Public Leadership**
    - In India and the U.S., private companies lead AI innovation.
    - In Finland and Singapore, governments set the pace.
4. **Global South vs. Global North**
    - Developing nations use AI to overcome resource shortages.
    - Wealthier nations focus more on personalization and advanced analytics.

Lessons for the Future

- **No One-Size-Fits-All:** Each country's strategy reflects local values and constraints.
- **Equity Must Be Central:** Without equity, AI risks widening global education gaps.
- **Partnerships Are Key:** Collaboration between governments, private companies, and NGOs drives success.
- **Ethics Cannot Be Ignored:** Nations that neglect privacy and fairness risk backlash and mistrust.

The Global Horizon

Looking ahead, international collaboration will be critical. AI in education is not just a local issue—it is a global one. Questions of equity, ethics, and sustainability require shared frameworks. Organizations like UNESCO, OECD, and the World Bank are beginning to push for global standards, but much work remains.

Key Takeaway

Global case studies reveal both the promise and the peril of AI in education. From China's scale to Finland's equity, from India's leapfrogging to Rwanda's innovation, the diversity of approaches shows that AI is not a single story—it is many.

The most important lesson is this: technology reflects values. The choices nations make about AI in education will shape not only learning outcomes but also the kind of societies students grow up in.

Vision for the Next Decade

The story of AI in education is still being written. In the past few years, we have seen a rapid shift from experimental tools to widespread adoption: automated grading, adaptive learning, predictive analytics, and AI-powered communication systems. But these are only the early chapters. The question now is: **where is this all going?**

By 2035, education may look radically different. AI will not simply supplement teaching; it will reshape how we define learning, assessment, and even the role of schools in society. The choices made over the next decade—about equity, ethics, and human purpose—will determine whether AI becomes a tool of empowerment or division.

The Classroom of 2035

Imagine a day in the life of a student in 2035:

- **Personalized Learning Pathways**
  Instead of rigid grade levels, students follow individualized pathways. AI tutors track their progress, offering lessons at the right difficulty, adjusting pace, and linking subjects across disciplines.

- **Seamless Human-AI Collaboration**
  Teachers act as mentors and facilitators, while AI handles administrative tasks, grading, and data analysis. Human interaction remains central, but AI provides real-time insights into student needs.
- **Immersive Environments**
  Science classes take place in VR labs where students experiment with molecules or travel through ecosystems. History lessons happen in augmented reality, blending narrative with firsthand exploration.
- **Emotionally Aware Systems**
  AI detects student frustration or disengagement, alerting teachers or adjusting learning strategies instantly.
- **Continuous Assessment**
  Exams are replaced by ongoing AI-driven assessments embedded in daily learning, reducing stress and capturing a fuller picture of growth.

This vision is not speculative fiction—many of these technologies already exist in early forms. By 2035, they could be mainstream.

The Teacher's Role in the Future

Contrary to fears of replacement, the next decade is likely to **elevate the role of teachers**, not eliminate it. With AI handling routine tasks, teachers will focus more on mentorship, creativity, and human connection.

Teachers will:

- Guide students in navigating ethical dilemmas.
- Foster collaboration and empathy.
- Help students interpret AI feedback critically.
- Design learning experiences that balance human and machine strengths.

The future teacher is not less important, but more essential—as the human anchor in an increasingly digital world.

The Student Experience

Students in 2035 will grow up as "AI natives." For them, AI tutors, adaptive platforms, and intelligent feedback systems will feel as natural as textbooks once did.

The risk, however, is **over-dependence**. Students may come to rely on AI too heavily, losing resilience or independent thinking. Schools must therefore teach not only how to use AI but also when not to use it.

Critical thinking, creativity, and ethical judgment will remain the most valuable skills—because they cannot be outsourced to machines.

Global Trends Shaping the Future

Several global forces will shape how AI in education evolves:

1. **Demographics**
    - Aging populations in countries like Japan will push AI as a solution to teacher shortages.
    - Growing youth populations in Africa and South Asia will demand scalable AI solutions for access.
2. **Economic Pressures**
    - Governments will seek AI to reduce costs and improve efficiency.
    - Private EdTech companies will drive innovation but also raise concerns about commercialization.
3. **Ethics and Regulation**
    - The EU's AI Act and similar policies will set global benchmarks.
    - Debates over surveillance, privacy, and fairness will intensify.
4. **Technology Integration**
    - Advances in VR, generative AI, and brain-computer interfaces will open new possibilities.

- Cloud-based ecosystems will link schools globally, sharing resources and analytics.

Opportunities for the Next Decade

1. **Universal Access to Education**
   AI could make high-quality education available to billions, including underserved rural and low-income communities.
2. **Closing Equity Gaps**
   With careful design, AI could provide targeted support to disadvantaged students, leveling the playing field.
3. **Personalized Lifelong Learning**
   Adults could retrain continuously through AI-powered platforms, reducing the risk of job displacement.
4. **New Pedagogies**
   AI may encourage schools to move beyond rote memorization, focusing on creativity, collaboration, and problem-solving.

Risks and Challenges Ahead

1. **Widening Inequality**
   Without equitable access, AI could deepen divides between wealthy and poor schools, countries, and communities.
2. **Surveillance and Privacy**
   Emotion-sensing systems and biometric monitoring risk creating schools of constant surveillance.
3. **Loss of Human Connection**
   Overuse of AI could devalue the teacher-student relationship, making learning feel transactional.
4. **Ethical Drift**
   Without strong policies, education could be shaped by corporate profit motives rather than human values.

Global Vision: Education by 2035

Different regions will pursue different futures:

- **North America & Europe:** Balanced adoption with strong regulation, focusing on equity and ethics.
- **Asia:** Rapid, large-scale adoption, particularly in China, though with risks of surveillance-heavy models.
- **Africa & South Asia:** Leapfrogging through mobile-based AI learning, if infrastructure improves.
- **Latin America:** Hybrid adoption, balancing affordability with innovation.

The most important question: will AI become a tool of **liberation** or **control**?

A Human-Centered Future

For AI in education to fulfill its promise, the next decade must prioritize:

- **Ethics:** Ensuring fairness, transparency, and respect for privacy.
- **Equity:** Guaranteeing all students—not just the wealthy—benefit from AI.
- **Empowerment:** Teaching students not just to use AI but to question and shape it.
- **Partnership:** Blending machine intelligence with human judgment, never replacing one with the other.

Key Takeaway

By 2035, AI will be woven into the fabric of education worldwide. The classroom of the future will be more personalized, immersive, and data-driven than anything we have seen before. But the true measure of success will not be technological—it will be human.

If we use AI to empower teachers, uplift students, and expand access, the next decade could mark a golden era of education. If we neglect ethics and equity, it could entrench divisions and erode trust.

The vision is clear: AI must serve humanity, not replace it. The future of education is not machines teaching humans—it is humans and machines learning together.

Glossary of Key Terms

Adaptive Learning
An instructional method powered by AI that adjusts the difficulty, pacing, and type of content based on each student's performance and needs.

Algorithm
A set of rules or instructions that a computer follows to solve problems or make decisions. In AI, algorithms process data to generate predictions, classifications, or recommendations.

Artificial Intelligence (AI)
A branch of computer science focused on creating systems that can perform tasks typically requiring human intelligence, such as problem-solving, pattern recognition, or natural language understanding.

Automated Assessment
The use of AI to grade assignments, evaluate tests, or provide feedback on student work without direct human intervention.

Bias in AI
When an AI system produces unfair results because of flawed or incomplete data, biased design choices, or reinforcement of historical inequalities.

Big Data
Extremely large datasets that can be analyzed by AI to reveal patterns, trends, and predictions—especially useful in personalized education.

Brain-Computer Interface (BCI)
A technology that enables direct communication between the human brain and digital systems, potentially useful for supporting students with disabilities or enhancing cognitive training.

Chatbot
An AI-powered virtual assistant that communicates with users through text or voice to answer questions or provide information.

Data Privacy
The right of individuals to control how their personal information is collected, stored, and used—especially critical in education, where sensitive student data is involved.

Deep Learning
A type of AI based on neural networks that can learn from massive amounts of data, often used in image recognition, speech processing, and adaptive learning platforms.

EdTech (Educational Technology)
Any technology—digital platforms, apps, or devices—designed to support teaching and learning. AI-powered EdTech refers to tools that use artificial intelligence to enhance education.

Emotionally Intelligent AI
AI systems designed to detect and respond to human emotions, often through analyzing voice, facial expressions, or physiological signals.

Equity in Education
Ensuring that all students—regardless of background, income, or identity—have access to fair and supportive learning opportunities.

FERPA (Family Educational Rights and Privacy Act)
A U.S. law protecting the privacy of student education records, limiting who can access and share them.

Generative AI
AI systems capable of creating new content such as text, images, music, or video. Examples include tools that generate essays, lesson plans, or learning materials.

GDPR (General Data Protection Regulation)
A European Union law that gives individuals strong rights over their

personal data, including consent and transparency requirements, relevant to education AI systems.

Learning Analytics
The use of data and AI to analyze student performance and engagement, helping teachers and institutions make better decisions.

Machine Learning (ML)
A subset of AI where systems improve performance over time by learning from data instead of being explicitly programmed.

MOOC (Massive Open Online Course)
An online course designed to support large-scale participation, often using AI to manage thousands of learners.

Natural Language Processing (NLP)
A branch of AI focused on enabling machines to understand, interpret, and generate human language. Used in AI tutors, translation tools, and chatbots.

Predictive Analytics
The use of AI models to forecast future outcomes, such as which students are at risk of dropping out or which interventions are likely to succeed.

Proctoring Software
AI tools used to monitor students during online exams, often through webcams or keystroke analysis. These systems raise debates about fairness, accuracy, and privacy.

Resource Allocation (AI in Education)
The use of AI to optimize how schools distribute resources such as staff, budgets, and learning materials to meet student needs efficiently.

Surveillance in Education
The monitoring of student behavior through AI systems, such as facial recognition or emotion tracking. A controversial practice raising ethical concerns.

Transparency (AI Ethics)
The principle that schools, teachers, and AI developers should clearly explain how AI systems work, what data they use, and how decisions are made.

Virtual Reality (VR)
A simulated digital environment that immerses students in interactive experiences, often enhanced by AI to personalize learning.

Well-Being Analytics
AI systems designed to monitor student stress, engagement, or emotional health, with the aim of improving mental well-being in education.

Thank You

Thank you for joining me on this journey into the future of education and artificial intelligence. I truly hope this book has given you fresh insights, sparked new ideas, and inspired you to think differently about how AI can shape learning for the better.

If you found value in these pages, I would be deeply grateful if you could take a moment to leave a review. Your feedback not only helps me grow as a writer but also helps other readers discover this book.

Your voice makes a difference—thank you for being part of this conversation about the future of education.

-Eric LeBouthillier